Engage, Empower, Energize

Engage, Empower, Energize

Leading Tomorrow's Schools Today

Dr. Robert Dillon

ROWMAN & LITTLEFIELD
Lanham • Boulder • New York • London

Published by Rowman & Littlefield
A wholly owned subsidiary of The Rowman & Littlefield Publishing Group, Inc.
4501 Forbes Boulevard, Suite 200, Lanham, Maryland 20706
www.rowman.com

16 Carlisle Street, London W1D 3BT, United Kingdom

British Library Cataloguing in Publication Information Available

Library of Congress Cataloging-in-Publication Data Available

Dillon, Robert, 1974–

Engage, empower, energize : leading tomorrow's schools today / Robert Dillon.
pages cm.
Includes bibliographical references.
ISBN 978-1-4758-0685-4 (cloth : alk. paper) — ISBN 978-1-4758-0686-1 (pbk.   ) —
ISBN 978-1-4758-0687-8 (electronic) 1. Educational leadership. I. Title.
LB2805.D5215 2014
371.2—dc23
                                                                                2014016087

Printed in the United States of America

Contents

Preface

School leaders, teachers, and those who surround the work of education are in a difficult space. The demands to achieve are higher than ever. The needs of kids, both academically and in the other spaces of their lives, are growing in intensity and complexity, while the resources needed to support them are growing narrower in scope. Resources include both the money used to run schools, and also the people and ideas used to feed schools. It is true that teachers and school leaders are working harder than ever, and for most, the work rate is reaching a breaking point. This is creating an unsustainable system.

In addition, the metrics of success are often a moving target. Educators see the goalposts as either moving, invisible, or always under construction. Even with these difficulties, schools are working to get better each day, but unfortunately, this idea of working to get better may actually be the greatest limiting factor on education today. A shift, with the potential to transform the learning spaces throughout the country, can only come from voices around the country demanding different.

Different schools are the ones that everyone wants their kids to attend. Different schools wouldn't allow someone to return from the moon after fifty years and still recognize learning as he or she knew it. Different schools are maximizing the learning and growth of both the students and adults using the passions and strengths that they bring to the table. Different schools aren't taking more tests, but they are testing solutions to the real-life problems that surround them each day. Different schools aren't about raising scores by 1 or 2 percent each year by wasting instructional time with test prep and unneeded benchmarking tests.

Thinking about different schools is scary, and they are even scarier to lead in a time when it is easier to manage the school and hide in the camouflage of mediocrity that surrounds today's schools. Being with innovative people in innovative spaces that are building allies and networks is a place of hope for those demanding different schools. Different schools, though, won't be demanded around the country until we solve the gap—not the achievement gap, but the courage gap. Education has a courage gap as educators are more risk-adverse than most professions. It takes courage to lead a school that goes about its business differently.

It takes courage to explain to parents that the honor roll assembly, the rewards, and the token economies are failing our kids. Because in a world where most of their children will be small business owners, self-employed, and entrepreneurs, external motivation doesn't get the job done. It takes courage to leverage the resources in an organization that embolden a larger mission while knowing that it will disrupt the inertia and happiness of many.

The schools that we need demand different. They need to support the open and transparent world that is exploding around education. This begins with pushing students into the center of the ring. In the center, there is no room to hide. It is a place of full engagement where real questions about real issues are being addressed with real solutions that will impact real people. Different schools are real. Different schools are life, and different schools breathe life into the students they serve.

The truth is communities, and this includes the global community, are demanding different, and the volume of our busyness to get better is drowning out the plea. The cat is out of the bag, but schools, for the most part, are trapped in the darkness of the bag. Demanding different means saying no to the industrial testing complex that surrounds the schools of today. It means being sensible about how to showcase learning for the teachers looking to shape new learning experiences as well as the external audiences. It means saying no to testing for the sake of testing, and it means creating excellence without the definition of excellence coming from the tip of a number two pencil.

It is easy to call for different, even to demand different, but how do educators go about crafting different? It begins with three words: engage, empower, energize. These three words should be the mission of all schools. Teachers and leaders that engage, empower, and energize will work tirelessly to push student choice, student voice, and authentic audience into daily learning. They will use these areas as the barometer of rigor and relevance. If they don't exist, it isn't good enough. Without these elements, the incrementalism of getting better creeps back into the equation, and the possibility of schools that are different becomes the dream of only a few.

Pockets of excellence exist, and they are available for replication. They are usually found in classrooms where teachers are demanding different. They are hiding in plain sight in schools seeking only better. In these spaces, students are connecting to their community by learning beyond the classroom. This may be learning at the beach or in the mountains, or their community connection can come from being in the backyard or a public park. Schools that are thinking different are finding ways to balance green time and screen time for kids. Kids are more naturally connecting through technology, so there is a need for balance with community connection.

In other spaces, those demanding different are engaging, empowering, and energizing learning through the power of story. Every job, every career, every space in life requires understanding the story of others, crafting a coherent narrative of one's own life, and telling the story of the ideas that are worth spreading. Different schools are telling their stories in a poignant, coherent, concise, and beautiful way each day because the community knows better schools, but the community needs help marrying itself to different schools.

It means that students are the storytellers of their learning, teachers are the storytellers of their spaces of learning, and school leaders play the role of storyteller in chief. Someone is always telling the story of the school. The storyteller, when done differently, should create such a cacophony coming from the inside that it is impossible for external forces to guide the story in the wrong direction. Different schools know that stories connect humans, and that all stories form an ecosystem that makes sense of the world. Different schools make sense for students.

Different schools are making. They are designing and creating in ways that push student passions to the forefront. The design thinking process is foundational to making. It surges empathy into schools and allows for students to begin to develop their brand. When students have their creations (writing, music, video, inventions) in places for purchase for an audience around the planet, they have no time to tarnish their digital footprint.

They realize that every Tweet, Facebook post, and picture on Instagram could be seen by a potential customer. Making allows for greater student understanding of marketing, economics, and more. Different schools are demanding that their students are passionate enough to creative, willing to risk failure, and bold enough to demand their place in the world. The best schools, not the ones trying to get better, are nesting learning in a way that eliminates silos, grows connections, and brings creation, collaboration, communication, and critical thinking to the heart of the work.

This isn't happening with a focus on school schedules, earning credits, and having bells to dictate when learning stops. Demand that the chains of schools that have served yesterday release their bonds. Lean into the possibility that being a part of a different type of school will make you infinitely more hirable in the future. Embrace the power to amplify the work of not only the school at which you park your car each day, but all schools, as the connections and networks are ready for this to happen. Say yes more often. Close the courage gap. Be willing to work different, think different, and serve different.

Demand different schools that engage, empower, and energize today's kids, who are our everything for tomorrow.

Acknowledgments

Being able to share ideas, thoughts, and resources with a much larger educational audience requires a degree of perseverance and inspiration that is hard to spark alone. It has taken two distinct groups of support to make this book possible. The first group has supported my work by providing acts of encouragement, showcasing work ethic by example, and helping me find the right balance between work and play. Most of them know who they are as they are my support team in life as well as in writing.

The second group is my personal learning network. In tough moments, when the momentum of education seems to be headed in a direction completely opposed to my philosophy, this network provides me with an armor to continue to do what is right for kids, which includes many of the ideas in this book. This group also provides daily inspiration and energy to put my ideas into action. Words alone can't begin to say thank you at the level needed to showcase my deep appreciation, but for now, I'll attempt to allow them to do just that. *Thank You.*

Introduction

This book travels two parallel tracks, with the story of Brad, a principal who is undergoing a reemergence from manager to leader, in one track, and the resources and ideas needed to bring high student engagement and student-centered work to the core of the mission of schools in the other track. It comes to readers in alternating chapters as the ten areas to engage, empower, and energize are brought to life. The design is based on the need to both envision and feel change through the narrative of a school leader in which many readers can relate, as well as have the structures and tools available to make that change.

Too often, books, lectures, articles, and blog posts attempt to create change by being persuasive to the head or the heart while leaving the other to chance, but the complex nature of change doesn't afford the option of tapping into one and not the other. The hope is that this book can enrich the conversation on the needed changes in education. The changes that place the soul of the child in the center by painting a picture of what is possible where culture, courage, and capacity are amplified with transformational and servant leadership.

The stories and examples in this book come from the experiences and dreams of those throughout education. Incredible learning takes place throughout the country every day, and there is a growing need to release the trapped wisdom of our classrooms and schools into the educational marketplace of ideas. This book is a small contribution to sharing what is right about education. The hope is to flood future learning spaces with engaged students who are thinking about how to solve the problems of the world.

ONE

Wandering into Safety

There wasn't a day or a moment. It just happened. The desire to lead just disappeared. It may have been the pressure of new standards or the intensity of the social commentary about how we should be competing with China and Finland. It could have been friends telling Brad over and over and over that he was spending too many hours in a profession that brought no recognition, honor, or glory. It may have just been fatigue—the fatigue that comes from introducing new ideas and innovative ways to engage and excite kids only to be ignored or given another set of data to analyze.

The bad part was that no one noticed, not even Brad, for almost four years. Brad had devolved into a school manager. Every piece of true energy to lead had disappeared from his body and soul, and no one noticed. Brad actually received a number of awards for his work as a manager. There were small bonuses for keeping the budget in order, praise for having a clean building, and every event on the checklist happened every year. His bosses rarely received a call complaining about his work. Brad did not bring work home with him, and he felt good.

Brad's school maintained its level of achievement on state tests for a number of years. There was nothing shocking in the numbers. Scores would rise one year and level off the next. The narrative to explain the data could always be built around new teachers, new curriculum, or new student transfers to the building. The community saw the school as a safe place for kids. Kids played youth league soccer on its fields, and families used the playground on a nice day. The school also had an active parent organization that served those in the community in need by providing coats and backpacks, and the school's annual canned food drive filled the local food pantry.

The staff at Brad's school slowly lost the "fire in their belly" that had propelled them into the profession to change the world. It wasn't that Brad didn't support their efforts, but teaching with passion means trying new things, advocating for the invisible, pushing back against the status quo, and entering into the cycle of fail, revise, fail, revise more frequently, and there was no sense of urgency to do any of those things from the community or from Brad. He knew that he was secure. The school was moving along without a hitch, and the energy it would take to move things in a new direction would mean disequilibrium and tons of energy both of which no longer seemed of interest to Brad.

Brad lived a comfortable life. His house was big enough for him and his dog, and it provided a place for his things, room to escape, and a chance to host friends for holidays and the big game. Brad was an avid rower. The local crew served as his social circle outside of education. He spent many hours building his endurance and strength so that he could compete on a local and regional level. He enjoyed the competition, and it fed his drive for success.

At times, though, Brad pictured a different life, one that he saw each day in the families that he served. He thought that he would be the dad on the sidelines at youth basketball games and that he would teach his son or daughter how to ride a bike, but those moments never materialized. He filled this slight regret with the freedom to explore and experience life to the fullest. Brad travelled often, taking trips overseas, visiting beach paradises, and enjoying adventures in the mountains to ski and soak in the crisp air.

Brad was no longer leading from his heart or his head; he was simply led by the inertia of the day. It wasn't until a chance meeting at the airport in Philadelphia that Brad would feel a discomfort about his work, his life, and his place on the planet. Brad was catching up on a recent education publication on his tablet when the person sitting next to him commented that he must work at a school. Brad politely responded that he was a principal of a school in Delaware and that he was travelling to visit his family in the Midwest.

Brad was hoping to maintain his airport anonymity and slide back into his reading, but the woman next to him continued by thanking Brad because she was sure that he was changing lives and giving kids new opportunities like those that had been provided to her when she was young. She continued by telling Brad that she was sure that he didn't want to hear her story. Brad politely ask her to continue as he knew that the solitude of travelling alone was gone for now anyway.

She introduced herself as Rena Sanchez, a proud single mother of two (Jonathan and Julia) who worked as an assistant in a local social work organization in Philadelphia that served children and families in crisis. Rena explained that the road to this "incredible life filled with daily opportunities to change the world" was made possible by three educators that she wished could see her now. Rena's mother carried her across a river when she was two, escaping a life in Mexico that was filled with the suffering of generational poverty and, for her mother, the physical and emotional abuse from Rena's dad. Rena's mom knew a few families living in a town about ten miles from the border.

They would knock on the door and hope that a fresh opportunity existed on the other side. It was a very communal beginning, four families living in a "house." The older girls would take turns skipping school to watch the younger kids while the four mothers worked in the shadows to make money for groceries. A small thirteen-inch television was the prime source of the children's early language instruction. With fear in their hearts, each of the young girls would head to the local school at the age of five.

On the first day in a new "scary" school, Rena walked into the classroom and into the arms of the sweetest woman on earth, Mrs. Ellis. Mrs. Ellis opened the doors of possibility by teaching her a new language and a passion and love for reading. She was masterful in loving Rena, pushing Rena, and knowing what Rena needed next. Mrs. Ellis bought her supplies, clothes, and small presents that she was sure that the other kids didn't get. She stopped for a moment and pulled Brad out of the vivid pictures of the story to say, "I can tell already that you care about kids in the same way." Rena then talked about her middle school counselor, Mr. Rias.

She described him as a gentle man who knew how to get to the point and through the smokescreen of the teenage years. Mr. Rias had a background similar to Rena's, and he knew that as many of her friends would slip into some social habits that could put Rena's dreams at risk. It was essential to keep her focused on what was possible. Rena said that the time with Mr. Rias was short as her family moved to Missouri where her mother and stepfather took jobs at a chicken processing plant. Mr. Rias still talks with Rena. He never stopped wondering about her, hoping for her, and caring about her. Rena emphasized, "It is amazing how one conversation, one act of kindness, one well-placed piece of advice sticks to kids."

As Brad heard this story, he asked himself when was the last time that he impacted a student or a family in this way. He had remembered early in his career doing the little extra things, but now he assumed that most of that was being done by his teachers and counselors.

Rena told Brad that she had to catch a flight soon, but she couldn't leave him before telling him about Dr. Turner. Dr. Turner was her AP History teacher in high school. She said that she had no business in AP History, but Dr. Turner insisted on her taking the class. She figured that it was from all the moments in freshman civics that she spent discussing how unfair our government was and how she was going to fix it someday. Dr. Turner planned one trip each year for his AP History class, and her trip was to Philadelphia.

Rena told Brad that there was no way that she would be where she was today without that trip and Dr. Turner. She talked about how she fell in love with Philadelphia, the college campuses, the smell of a real city, and the opportunity to fix the government where government started. Rena finished her story about Dr. Turner by looking at Brad and telling him to make sure that he has many teachers like Dr. Turner in his school, and that she hopes to visit his school someday and see the incredible ways that he is changing the lives of kids.

Rena left Brad, but Rena's story never left him. He knew that Monday would need to be different. He wanted back in the game of changing kids' lives.

QUESTIONS FOR REFLECTION

What would your reaction have been if someone approached you in the airport to tell you their story?

Where in your leadership have you slipped into an area of managing instead of leading?

In what ways do you connect with Brad, the school leader in chapter 1?

TWO

The Roadmap

The journey from leader to manager and back to leader that began in chapter 1 is rare for leaders in education these days as it takes a tremendous amount of courage. The inertia that moves leaders from passionate visionary to worthy manager is strong. Very often the pressure from rules, regulations, and the desire for job security takes over. The title of this book almost became The Courage Gap because this gap is the one that educators, especially educational leaders, need to truly examine if they want to solve the other "gaps" that plague the educational system.

Courage for a leader is talked about, written about, but rarely practiced at the level necessary for change. Courage is tiring, exhausting, and filled with professional potholes. The fruits of courage, though, are actually a chance to make a difference, not in the way that gives leaders just enough stories over their career to call themselves a success, but the kind of difference that can transform a system and create a legacy of excellence for future leaders to follow. The kind of difference that builds a greater capacity for the changing needs of our struggling system of public education.

This book isn't about the right answers or a silver bullet, but a collection of practices that are known to get kids excited about their learning. They give students choice, voice, authentic audience, and opportunities to make change. They engage students' bodies, minds, and souls. Not every school will be ready for all of these ideas. Not every school is right for these ideas, but innovation, risk, and the road to excellence begins by building a coalition of courage with leaders, teachers, and students as a part of the planning.

Schools looking to be different and not just better need leaders that are ready to lead and not manage. Leaders that know that discomfort and change are the new norm will excel, and students who have an opportunity to grow in these engaging environments will change the world as it is known today.

Chapters 3 through 6 look at the idea of the permeable classroom and the growth possible when educators tune into the natural ecosystems that surround students. Many schools are finding ways for students to learn outside of the classroom in their community, and these experiences for students are high engagement moments when all of their senses are awakened. Beyond the traditional classroom field trip, the opportunities described in these chapters are rich expeditionary learning experiences that require careful planning before, during, and after the experience. Students that are learning beyond the classroom have a natural connection to the interconnected nature of the elements in their surroundings.

By tapping into this connection, students have an incredible opportunity to think about concepts like the triple bottom line of profits, people, and planet as well as how the concepts of social justice, economic justice, and environmental justice play into their growth as citizens. The concepts surrounding Education for Sustainability provide students with a greater context for their learning and go to the heart of answering the age-old student question, "why are we learning this?" In addition, Education for Sustainability provides students with one of the key catalysts for engagement, the opportunity to make change in their community, country, and beyond.

Chapters 7 through 10 examine two spaces for providing student choice. Student choice has continually proved to be a strong element in the schools where engagement is of foremost importance. The first part of this section looks at the promise and power of technology integration. As schools couple a strong broadband infrastructure with quality teacher development in this space, they are able to deliver instruction to students that is personal. This allows freedom in how students showcase their learning and focuses instruction on the four essentials of quality technology integration: creation, collaboration, communication, and critical thinking.

Schools are also finding success in engaging students with a variety of project-based learning opportunities. Project-based learning allows students to dive deeply into experiences that are molded around learning standards, and it features student choice in how learning is showcased. The best practices of project-based learning also insert an element of authentic audience into the mix, which keeps the teacher's desk from being the final resting place for the excellent work produced by the students. The idea of student choice has been in the best schools for a long time, and it continues to drive engagement for kids who haven't found their place in the formal learning systems that surround them.

Chapters 11 through 14 explore learning through examining mental models and the use of story and narrative. Students want to have their voice heard, and they want to know both the origin of their voice and how to grow it into a space that allows it to be heard by larger audiences. To do so, these chapters show how bringing systems thinking tools into the classroom can develop a common language for conversations surrounding how ideas and concepts are connected. It also looks at how the systems change over time, and how mental models lie below thoughts, beliefs, and assumptions.

Systems thinking in education opens the doors to incredibly rich conversations surrounding complex and interconnected topics. It allows students to struggle with ideas, beliefs, and assumptions, and it unlocks a way for students to support their ideas by using the characteristics of a systems thinker. The global economic marketplace is a rapidly growing system that requires a savvy learner to navigate its complexity, and the use of systems thinking in schools has shown to not only promote student voice (by providing the language needed to formulate ideas), but it provides students with a mindset for observing and acting on any problem that the world may place in their path.

This section also looks at the power of story: how telling stories brings strength to places of learning, how it emboldens grit and perseverance, and how it binds a community of learners. It outlines how teachers can demonstrate the power of story by making sure that their personal stories of hard work, dedication, and quest for excellence aren't invisible.

Allowing story to permeate a school provides students with incredible opportunities for their voice to be heard, which again fosters engagement. It also gives students a safe place to figure out what they believe, express it in words, rethink their ideas, and present their thoughts for a larger audience. Working on the power of story also creates a space for the concepts of digital citizenship and a digital footprint to come alive for students.

Chapters 15 through18 examine how schools and communities are an ecosystem that can work together to prepare students to be productive citizens. Many schools struggle to thin the walls of their classrooms to a point where they are learning deeply from the experts in the community. Schools need to maximize how they weave both the human and natural resources of the community into daily learning.

These chapters outline how teachers can facilitate learning through service to the community as well as projects that provide students an opportunity to solve problems that are real to the community. This means students working side by side with government officials and community agencies to generate some of the best solutions in the room.

The taxpayers of every community want to know that there is quality education in their schools, and every school has a responsibility to demonstrate what excellent education looks like. By thinning the school walls, the community gathers trust in the school while holding it accountable for the right stuff. The thin walls allow the community to visualize excellent learning while at the same time shift their mental models of schooling.

These chapters dive deeply into the concept of citizen science, which has the ability to maximize engagement in all learners. It looks at a number of the citizen science projects that exist around the world and how teachers and leaders can build learning around data collection and analysis, the scientific method, and advocacy for issues through participation in these projects. Citizen science is a way for kids to feel like they are contributing to something larger than themselves in a meaningful way.

Citizen science projects bring students outside of the classroom to gather data and specimens and discuss issues of science with local advocacy groups and experts. It can even be an avenue to connect classrooms with similar passions around the world. Students that aren't trapped behind classroom doors, building walls, or school fences have a rich field of learning in front of them in both their local and global communities.

Chapters 19 through 22, the final chapters, discuss two types of "making," the change making that is possible through building a culture of empathy, and the potential of the maker movement that seems poised to grow a new generation of design thinkers and fill the niche of right-sized manufacturing in this country. Schools are beginning to see the incredible energy that comes from having students showcase their learning through the use of design thinking, hi-tech manufacturing tools, and fresh processes that unleash students to connect their hands and minds.

The ideas for today's makerspaces rise out of some of the best practices that schools have been using over the last fifty years, including woods, metals, and drafting classes, but the new maker movement is doing an excellent job of wrapping together the power of creation with some of the tools and software needed for a shrinking job market that demands unique skills and creativity. It is amazing to watch kids working in these spaces; the focus, the attention to detail, and the interest in doing draft after draft.

The other making in this section deals with change making. Our society is ripe for big change. We have to soon feed ten billion people, make sure that there is potable water for the planet, and secure enough energy to handle the next global middle class. These are daunting problems that will take big, audacious answers, and the students of today will be in the middle of those challenges creating solutions.

Finding solutions often means finding the right problems to solve. Finding the right problems to solve requires deep empathy. How can you help others solve the problems of their space if you don't have empathy? Students need opportunities to practice empathy from the youngest of ages, beginning with their siblings and classmates before growing to their teachers, other adults, and the community that surrounds them.

Schools that are looking to engage students deeply need to showcase their empathy for kids as well as showcase how empathy building occurs. Empathy doesn't come from always being comfortable and not asking the tough questions. Empathy has a ripple of positive, unintended consequences for schools and the children that they are serving.

QUESTIONS FOR REFLECTION

In what learning spaces do you see students most engaged?

Which of the ideas outlined above gives you the most pause when thinking about trying it in your school? Why?

What is one idea that you are currently using in an innovative way that didn't make it into the book?

THREE

A Walk in the Park

Walking in the park, Brad realized his recent decision to provide his students more experiences outside of the classroom was starting to change how he lived. His time in the park on Saturday morning was becoming the norm. It was his recalibration for the week. It was his way to cleanse the palette from the grind of the previous week.

Brad was starting to actually stop, unplug, and absorb the space around him. He heard the birds, noticed the soil under his feet, and his breathing was a part of his conscious decision making. For a guy that had been running at full throttle for years, this was a nice change. Brad realized that he needed time to go slow so that he could go fast. The shift for his students was welcomed by many of them almost immediately.

Brad worked with his teachers over the first summer to plan a trip for his students that would have them away from home for two nights during the school year. He had a grand vision for this type of programming that would have the students outside of their primary learning spaces 20 to 25 percent of the school year, meaning that they would be learning outside, out in the community, or outside of the community for one-quarter of the school year. He knew though that this would be a big shift for the teachers, students, and community. Brad wanted to work quickly to begin this process, but he also wanted to make sure that he was planning for success.

Failing around the edges in his first endeavor was inevitable, but a complete collapse on his first trip could set the program back for years. Brad had always longed to give his students an experience that rivaled the learning and fun that he had in the summer as a Boy Scout. Boy Scout camp for him provided some incredible experiences that shaped his love of the outdoors and his ability to persevere and overcome problems in less than ideal conditions.

He knew though that this type of experience was a current reality for only about 10 percent of his students as most of them spent their evenings and weekends in front of the television, playing video games, and living a sedentary lifestyle. Brad realized that there were a lot of additional advantages to getting his students out of the classroom to learn, including getting their bodies moving to support other classroom learning.

The energy surrounding planning the first trip was quite positive. Teachers wanted the opportunity to utilize the space around them, as they had passed up on so many opportunities in their careers that would have connected them to the community and their surroundings. In the past, the teachers knew that they could plan something like this, but they also knew that it was all on them. They would have to negotiate all of the hurdles, logistics, and road blocks that came from trying something innovative. Now that the school was supporting this way of learning, and teachers were ready to dive into the opportunity.

During the second planning meeting, reality set in. Teachers realized that they would be staying overnight supervising kids. They would be working twenty-four hours a day for three days, and they would need to build programming for the entire time. Brad worked to temper the worry by discussing the support system that would be available for the staff, including having parents and high school students join the trip, using staff on-site, and supplementing the teaching staff with other experts that could lead learning.

The trip took shape for Brad and his staff. They would be travelling to an area state park that had cabins, a dining hall, and plenty of green space for learning. The teachers spent some time prior to the trip talking with the students. On the surface, most of them were very excited to be doing something different than the norm of sitting in classrooms listening to teachers present material. They were excited for a new adventure. On the inside, they were nervous. Some of the students had never spent a night away from home, and many had never been in the woods at night.

These worries sat below the surface, but Brad knew that they a reality. He worked to remove as much of the fear as possible. He talked with students that seemed nervous or had not turned in their paperwork, and he also worked hard to explain the opportunity to his families. This was foreign territory for many of them as well. Many families were uncomfortable with having their children away from home as most had never had an experience like this as a child.

The first trip "happened." That was how Brad blogged about it upon his return. He went on to say that it was a learning experience and that the kids had a good time. Brad returned exhausted in a good way and learned a lot about how to better support teachers and kids in the future. The staff was tired as well, but most of them returned knowing that there was no going back. Teaching and learning were going to be different from this moment forward.

There were a few teachers that were pushed completely out of their comfort zone, and they voiced their objection to these trips. They called them a waste of time, outside of the scope of their contract, and not right for "this" group of kids. Most of the kids thanked Brad for the opportunity, but this didn't mean that there weren't some behavior issues on the trip. When kids are put in uncomfortable situations, they often push back with some misbehavior. Having students in bunk beds with their buddies seemed a lot more like a sleepover to some than a place to sleep before getting up to learn at 7 a.m.

Other students got extremely tired from the physical demands of walking from learning space to learning space throughout the day. Others struggled with learning spaces that had a different set of structures than the normal classroom. These issues didn't distract Brad as he returned from the trip. He was ready to expand his vision. During the trip, he saw deep learning, exploration, and investigation. He saw students connecting with their teachers in a new way. He witnessed the joy of learning and a growing community of learners ready to support each other.

Brad knew that this trip was an initial test drive and that there was a lot of fine-tuning to do. He wanted future trips to have three phases: learning and preparation for the trip, the trip itself, and reflection upon returning. In order to maximize the learning, the students needed to have a learning road paved prior to the trip and plenty of space to reflect once their senses had recalibrated and life returned to normal after their return.

Brad also knew that he needed to change the name of these experiences. The words that used education are powerful for giving meaning to the purpose of the moment. Brad would eventually call these experiences *learning expeditions*. Expedition, as a term, gave a sense of adventure and weight to the learning that was taking place.

Brad also began to hire different types of people to support this vision. Teachers could no longer think of themselves as subject area teachers but as teachers of the whole child that embraced the work and learning that happened on expeditions. A few of Brad's current staff resisted losing instructional time for their subject to take students on these trips. They didn't embrace the idea that expeditions allowed students to have context to their learning in all subjects. Some teachers didn't have a sense of adventure. For others, the idea of being away from their families for two or three days and sometimes a week was too much for them to embrace.

Each new hire and each new person that chose to move on brought fresh energy to the initiative as more and more capacity wrapped itself into the system. Students started to see this type of learning as a rite of passage, and younger brothers and sisters were excited about their chance for adventure in their learning.

Parents eventually embraced this core value of the school. They raised funds where necessary, provided supplies for students who didn't have them, and made room in their schedules to chaperone these events. Brad had created fresh energy in his space. It wasn't the easy thing to do. It wasn't the type of thing that Brad as a manager of the school would have done, but Brad was in a new space, one filled with a greater sense of urgency, one with a desire to lead, one with a desire to change the world.

QUESTIONS FOR REFLECTION

What decisions by Brad during this process did you see as essential?

What would you need to do differently in your school's culture to make this type of learning possible?

Brad chose for this initiative to be the first change. Would you have chosen differently?

FOUR

Experiencing Engagement

Life is a series of experiences, both small and large, and the potential to learn from each of them is tremendous. From attending a sporting event to observing the clover growing in the yard, there are unlimited ways to attach learning to experiences. Experiential learning is a natural way for students to grow and learn. To maximize each of these experiences, a guide is necessary, someone who has had this experience before, is deeply familiar with how the experience can be tied to other experiences, and can bring a perspective that stretches the current mental models of those experiencing this fresh opportunity. This role of guide is the foundational purpose of teaching.

Not all experiences are equal. A hike in a rainstorm is different from a hike on a beautiful sunny day, and the sounds of the orchestra in perfect rhythm is a different experience than the sounds of the neighborhood band playing at 1 a.m. Experiencing a team winning the Super Bowl, the World Series, or a national championship is a different experience from being present for a lackluster midseason loss. But there is value to all experiences, and there is learning to be had in all spaces at all times. The primary responsibility for educators in these moments is to craft a set of learning experiences that allows leaders, scholars, citizens, and stewards to emerge in their students.

Like no time in history, the learners on our planet have the opportunity to have experiences at the core of their formal education. These experiences can now come not only from being out in the community, but also through technology integration that connects students to the far corners of the globe. These experiences can also come from a greater desire by community partners to play an active role in the growth and education of students in the school walls.

These opportunities, however, aren't equal for all students. As educators have focused on the achievement gap between affluent students and students living in poverty, the lack of focus on the experience and opportunity gaps have created a chasm between the two groups, leaving students with the most resources at home with the richest set of experiences at school.

Closing these gaps is a moral imperative. Because without experiences, learning is muted, and muted learning significantly impacts the chances for students in poverty to be accepted into and succeed in college. All students need a rich set of learning experiences at school that move them beyond desks, rows, and the traditional classroom walls. Students that persevere through poverty at home shouldn't be subjected to daily learning that is void of the life-giving opportunities that come from experiential learning. Excellent experiential learning comes in many forms, but all of the experiences come with a set of intended learning outcomes.

This can happen in a number of ways, but most often this looks like students using their experiences to answer essential questions and grow in new ways surrounding rich enduring understandings. It also comes with the realization that other valuable learning will take place in an organic way that needs to be nurtured during the process. The teachers guiding these experiences have the responsibility of maximizing the individual engagement of all students, limiting the amount of time used for transitions, and administrative tasks, and promoting a learning energy surrounding the work.

Engagement is a catalyst for learning. When students have the opportunity to move beyond teacher-directed learning to student-led learning that is attached to experiencing something new, incredible growth occurs. The best teachers in this space build a culture of positive risk taking, have students supporting other students, and design structures that allow students to be present for the experiences in front of them. Experiential learning often can't be replicated as it is unique to the moment.

A service learning experience such as visiting the homeless shelter, surveying neighbors at the park on use of green space in the city, or planting lettuce in the raised bed garden are experiences that happen only once because the next moment in each of these spaces possesses different variables. It is essential for leaders and teacher leaders to have great energy surrounding the new experiences that they are providing the students. Most people are apprehensive about new experiences, and students experience these same emotions of not wanting to do something wrong, look silly in their learning, or fail.

Lead learners can help students overcome this nervous energy by showcasing their excitement about the opportunity to grow and learn in what lies ahead. Adult energy surrounding an experience can truly amplify the level of success a student achieves. Following the experience, expected and unexpected learning has taken place and students then have a fresh energy for learning. At this point, students should be directed back to the enduring understandings and essential questions so as to anchor the learning around the big ideas. Too often though, the temptation in many learning spaces is to quickly move forward in the name of curriculum coverage.

It is in this space that school leaders and teacher leaders need to remain resolute in cementing the learning that has just occurred through reflecting, sharing, and collaborating. This space can allow the strengths of all students to be tapped, by injecting a broader scope of their ideas across the learning space. This release of the trapped wisdom helps everyone to grow.

Leaders looking to begin this work should think about a variety of learning locations for students to experience their learning. Classrooms, when designed as places of exploration, can be a starting place for experiential learning. The key is that the experience needs to look and feel different from a normal day in the classroom. When a science teacher turns the classroom into a roller coaster factory for the day, learning is being experienced. Experiential learning must also take place outside of the classroom. This can be on campus, in a park, or out in the community.

Leaders should also consider taking students into spaces outside of the community. It grows concepts like empathy, understanding, and tolerance and magnifies the learning. Schools in the Expeditionary Learning Network have experienced the power of this learning, and they are finding ways to build robust experiential learning for kids. Their organization also has incredible resources and templates for designing and executing highly effective experiential learning opportunities for all kids, no matter the location of their classroom.

Some keys to beginning this work in schools include choosing an experience that one or more faculty member has energy for; developing before, during, and after learning strategies to surround the experience; and beginning sooner rather than later because the value of this mode of learning can only be truly recognized when it is experienced by adults.

QUESTIONS FOR REFLECTION

How could you see this engagement strategy influencing the learning for your school?

What current projects/ideas exist in your school that could be molded into a greater experience for kids?

What community partners could be available to support this work in your school?

RESOURCES

Expeditionary Learning, http://elschools.org/

Smith, M. K. (2001, 2010). "David A. Kolb on experiential learning," *The Encyclopedia of Informal Education,* http://infed.org/mobi/david-a-kolb-on-experiential-learning/

Wurdinger, Scott D. and Julie A. Carlson, *Teaching for Experiential Learning: Five Approaches That Work* (Lanham: Rowman & Littlefield Education, 2009).

Place-based Education, www.promiseofplace.org/

FIVE

Growing a Sustainable School

After bringing expeditionary learning into the culture of the school, Brad had an opportunity the following summer to work with a group of teachers from around the country that were interested in infusing the concepts of Education for Sustainability (EfS) into the curriculum. Brad was new to Education for Sustainability, but he had always thought that kids and communities needed to spend more time and resources on these concepts.

Brad remembered the stories that his dad told him about how the river near their home was so polluted by the factories upstream that fish were dying in mass and no one dared to swim in the river. This was the same river that Brad found himself training on each week, and it wasn't rare for him to fill his water bottle straight from the river as it was now known for its cleanliness. Brad realized that someone had taken a stand and advocated for change many years before he even knew that there were issues with the river, and he wanted to grow students with that same drive and mission.

The week-long work session brought Brad to a deeper understanding about the ideas and philosophy at the heart of Education for Sustainability. He moved from thinking about having his teachers and staff recycle more, turn off lights, and reduce food waste in the cafeteria to seeing how connecting social justice, economic justice, and environmental justice issues to the rich learning culture that was evolving at his school could lead to building his students into leaders, citizens, scholars, and stewards. Brad used this week to add another lens to his educational philosophy.

Education for Sustainability for Brad was now more of a way of thinking and acting as a leader than it was a checklist of things that were required to call his school an Education for Sustainability school. Brad

19

s space knowing that the concepts of justice, embedded in the heart ducation for Sustainability, matter deeply when building the type of chool that educators, parents, and students truly want. He was bolstered by the with new ideas and found himself in a most dangerous position as he returned to campus.

Upon his return, Brad itched to open up this new vault of ideas. He called a few teachers, and he invited them to lunch. He was going to build a cohort in his building that could help him to repackage the learning to revolve around the big, complex, and hairy ideas that come through the learning lens of Education for Sustainability. Brad was reading and preparing for the meeting. He knew the importance of the first meeting when it came to new ideas, and he was going to be ready to answer any of their questions. Brad was so glad to see Jane arrive early.

Jane was a passionate teacher. She fought for funding for the county library and started a bit of a ruckus in town about the new Walmart. She was the type of teacher that Brad was convinced would be overjoyed that her passion to be an active citizen could be cultivated in her classroom. Brad talked with her about his time at the conference. She seemed interested, but he wasn't getting the reaction that he expected. The other two teachers joining them for lunch came to the table in the middle of a discussion around the implications of the changes to the health care coverage by the school district.

Brad certainly had the passionate folks at the table. Just before he started his prepared opening on the importance of bringing the concepts of Education for Sustainability to the school, he stopped, paused, and realized that he was approaching this from totally the wrong way. Even though he had brought expeditionary learning to his staff with success, Brad realized that implementing Education for Sustainability needed to be different.

The topic of justice is very personal for most people. Some educators are ready to share their thoughts and actions in these spaces and other remain quite guarded. Brad knew that pushing the conversation into planning mode with these teachers in this moment could derail the student experience and may leave the power of student voice on the sidelines in a critical moment.

Brad wanted these passionate teachers facilitating Education for Sustainability, but he now realized that he wanted the passion, topics, and ideas to rise from his students. Brad turned the meeting into a listening session. It became an opportunity for him to hear about the adventures of his teachers over the summer, and there were also plenty of moments for his teachers to dive into the finer points of the district's medical insurance. Brad had one of those leadership by omission moments, and it potentially saved his desire to make Education for Sustainability a cornerstone of the learning at his school.

Brad saw a new opening in August when his student council returned to do some planning for the new school year. He asked for 45 minutes with the kids, and he worked with the sponsor on his plan. He wanted to build some student definitions around social, economic, and environmental justice. He then wanted the students to make a list of the issues that were most important to them under each area. The students compiled a lengthy list, but Brad had them narrow the list to a top five.

Once completed, Brad also talked with the students about how important these issues were to him. He talked about how issues of race and class had affected him growing up as a poor, white male, and at the same time acknowledged how much privilege he still had. He talked about the importance of serving the poor, and how he looked for ways to level the playing field for kids that had less. He told the kids that he never wanted poverty-related issues to keep any student from experiencing school the way that they should.

Finally, he told a story about how he dreamed of being a part of a solution surrounding one of the big issues of our planet. He dreamed about supporting efforts to have plentiful food and water for all people, and he wanted to make sure that we are creative in our solutions surrounding energy. Brad finished by saying that he was going to take the students' list to the teachers so that they could weave the students' passions into their units of study.

Since Brad had found new strength in leading his school, he vowed to make professional development and learning different in the building. He wanted teachers thinking and growing in as many spaces as possible. To begin this shift, he created a wall with all of the names of the units of study in all subjects, the concepts of Education for Sustainability, the list of topics in these areas that maximized student engagement, and the expeditionary learning opportunities already on the calendar. With all of this information, the staff started to make the connections necessary to plan the year.

Brad continued to bring them back to the ideas that the students had generated, and he pushed their thinking about the potential that Education for Sustainability could have in their classroom. In addition, he painted a picture for the staff that the work around Education for Sustainability wasn't about the teachers. Although their passion and energy surrounding these topics was essential, it was about building students that stood for something and being a school that was about growing a vibrant community.

Brad knew that fostering Education for Sustainability in his students was about creating common language, unpacking the complex concepts of Education for Sustainability, and having extensive opportunities to practice living sustainably. In addition, he was realizing with greater clarity that developing the processes, values, and ethics in a school on the journey to embracing Education for Sustainability took an incredible amount of time, talent, and resources. Brad had believed for a long time that his role was to build the basic literacy and numeracy skills in students so that they would be prepared for the rigors of high school, but this awakening that Brad was experiencing had him pushing for ways to support the development of good people as well as good students.

He remembered a teacher telling him a long time ago that you can be an A student and an F person, and he knew that he didn't want any of his students to be F people. Brad imagined that, over time, his students would be able to have more thoughtful conversations around the subject of racism and classism. He wanted his students to lean into the difficult conversations, learn how to disagree without being disagreeable, and build a habit of students knowing multiple angles to the same story.

Brad knew that poverty creates incredible friction in our society, but he never used the poverty of his students as an excuse. He knew though that it was an explanation for the struggles that his students experienced. Through Education for Sustainability, he hoped to build a greater sense of empathy for the students and families struggling with the effects of poverty, and he also wanted to empower students to act in these situations to stand up and speak up for those in need. Brad was certain that beyond the basic literacies was a literacy of the soul that allowed students to feel and think about those less fortunate no matter whether they reside in their community or around the world.

Year one was a mixed bag, but ultimately, Brad knew that a shift was beginning. There were more conversations around Education for Sustainability, and visible signs were starting to emerge. Students were using their choices on class projects to think and analyze topics surrounding people, planet, and pocketbook. Brad knew that these sorts of changes would take time. Though he came back to campus the previous summer passionate about making this an essential part of his school, he now knew that he would need to harness that energy as though he was running a marathon not a sprint.

Many of Brad's teachers talked with him about how they were energized to see students excited and passionate about topics even though the students thought quite differently at times from the teacher. Teachers also talked about bringing their passion for topics into the classrooms. They were able to talk about stories when they were advocates for causes and took risks to speak up when it was difficult.

Students were now pushing Brad on issues around the school. Why don't we recycle more? Isn't there too much food waste? How can we provide for more families in the community? Brad spent a lot of time working with students on these issues, empowering their ideas, and pushing them to think further. All of this time spent working through these questions fed his students, fed the culture of the school, and fed Brad's desire to lead his school and education to new places.

QUESTIONS FOR REFLECTION

When does a leader need to worry about his or her beliefs on ideas like Education for Sustainability being the wrong ones for his or her school?

What steps in this process could you replicate in your school?

How and when should students wrap into the change process in a school?

SIX

Engaging through Education for Sustainability

Building responsible students who have a global perspective requires a shift in language, resources, and actions. It is a shift from an orientation of valuing stuff to valuing experiences. This orientation shift for students and adults can be a very difficult one. It requires pushing back against the pressures of marketing, advertising, and the power of persuasion that play such a deep role in the decision-making paradigm of society.

Having and valuing stuff is deeply ingrained in the systems, traditions, and routines of our schools, communities, and societies. Ultimately, consumer spending remains the engine of the economy, and buying things and having stuff has become a yoke on the opportunity to grow a middle class here and abroad. Students who have a larger perspective when it comes to valuing experience as opposed to stuff can become active citizens capable of solving the big issues of our planet. Students who can grasp that the accumulation of stuff creates issues for people, the planet, and pocketbooks can begin to reshape their relationships with what is important to learn.

They can also see greater value in the types of experiences that can help them grow their potential to solve future problems. The principles of Education for Sustainability (EfS) and ecoliteracy, as outlined later in this chapter, grow student perspective, and they encourage deeper learning and engagement as students see the power to make immediate change in areas in which they are passionate.

The Cloud Institute for Sustainability Education has been working on this issue since 1995 under the leadership of Jamie Cloud and others, defines EfS as "a transformative learning process that equips students, teachers, and school systems with the new knowledge and ways of thinking we need to achieve economic prosperity and responsible citizenship

25

while restoring the health of the living systems upon which our lives depend." Schools around the globe have allowed this definition to guide their systems of learning, creating fresh energy and engagement for kids.

The Cloud Institute sees the journey for schools in the area of Education for Sustainability to include five interconnected parts that grow and evolve together. These include: the learning self; the learning classroom; schools that learn; physical plant, procurement, and investments; and communities that learn. Looking more deeply at each of these areas can provide leaders an opportunity to see where an entry point to Education for Sustainability may exist for their school.

The learning self encompasses the knowledge, skills, attitudes, and habits of mind that make it possible to live within the means of nature. For schools looking to grow in this area of the "learning self," it requires developing a common language surrounding sustainability and showcasing adult actions in these areas. It means putting on the oxygen mask of the adults in the area of Education for Sustainability before attempting to weave the concepts into the overall student instructional plan.

The capacity of schools grow in the next stage of the journey, the learning classroom. This is where high-quality instructional methodologies produce authentic and engaging learning. Teachers in this space, having spent time in a phase of self-learning, now have greater capacity and confidence to learn with students about EfS. Students are given additional opportunities to experience their learning, showcase their learning using student choice and student voice with an authentic audience, and reflect on the power of experience in their lives.

Schools that learn are about growing the organizational culture and structures that encourage innovation, collaboration, reflection, and self-correction. For schools, bringing concepts and ideas into classrooms is often the easy part of change. The sustainable part of leading change and placing something like Education for Sustainability at the core of an organization requires deep change. It means conversations with students, staff, and the community about how learning through Education for Sustainability can have great power. It means examining all of the structures of the organization through the lens of EfS to find ways to reduce the waste that negatively impact the people, paychecks, and planet across the system.

Physical plant, procurement, and investments is an aspect of EfS that is exemplified in the work of the book *The Third Teacher*. This book demonstrates, with elegance, the importance of students learning in healthy, beautiful spaces in order to spark learning, engagement, and passion for inquiry. School leaders shaping change in these spaces have an opportunity to positively contribute to the long-term health of economic, ecological, and social systems of their school and district.

Schools, reflecting about potential changes in this space, are often considering changes that lessen their ecological footprint through efforts by using more environmentally friendly cleaning products, improving air quality through better filters and ventilation, and creating conditions that maximize classroom acoustics. They are also thinking about how to support causes in their community that sync with the EfS mission in the schools.

The final piece of the Education for Sustainability journey for schools surrounds communities that learn. The best schools are permeable in that they are able to learn from the community and have the community learn with them. Though schools can be incubators for change surrounding the principles of Education for Sustainability, real change comes when students are engaged with community partners surrounding the concepts of social, economic, and environmental justice that are at the heart of EfS. Students, in these spaces, often provide fresh energy to community social structures that struggle to find urgency in solution making on key community needs.

Schools looking to grow in these areas can build on the work of the US Partnership for Education for Sustainable Development. This organization plays a variety of roles including having sector teams in communities, business, faith communities, K–12 and teacher education, and higher education. The work of the sector team for K–12 and teacher education has produced a strong blueprint for school leaders looking to implement the concepts of Education for Sustainability. The blueprint outlines age appropriate topics and concepts for the youngest of learners to those preparing for college and careers. The standards are based around three core concepts.

The first Education for Sustainability core standard in the blueprint is that students understand and are able to apply the basic concepts and principles of sustainability. The standards break this learning into seven components that have topics of study attached to them. The components are intergenerational responsibility, interconnectedness, ecological systems, economic systems, social and cultural systems, personal action, and collective action. Through these components, schools can begin to thread together a dialogue about the essential nature of sustainability as well as the complex nature of building dynamic systems.

In addition, within this framework, there is great freedom allowing schools to bring local issues and opportunities to the table. This creates the potential to maximize engagement and support additional passion-based learning for students. Examples of this could include students working with an area organization that supports human rights issues or schools bringing in expert mentors to work with students who are exploring the water quality of the neighborhood.

Education for sustainability is robust in its opportunities to help students create, connect, and collaborate in ways that allow them to embrace the tradition of the Iroquois Nation who attempted to make every decision with the knowledge that their actions would impact the next seven generations.

The second core standard is that students recognize the concept of sustainability as a dynamic condition characterized by the interdependency among ecological, economic, and social systems and how these interconnected systems affect individual and societal well-being. In pursuing proficiency in this standard, students develop an understanding of the human connection to and interdependence with the natural world. Building a sense of connection is central to sustainability and student engagement, and school leaders and teachers can foster this connection by linking students to other learners; connecting teachers and students through relationship; and threading ideas, concepts, and learning through interdisciplinary studies.

The themes of Education for Sustainability dovetail into these connection strategies. In addition, they can provide synergy and amplification for students trying to make sense of the world that surrounds them. The study of interconnectedness often creates more questions than answers, but the questions are rich, and engaging, and they create new areas for exploration for students and adults.

The final core standard around Education for Sustainability is that students develop a multidisciplinary approach to learning the knowledge, skills, and attitudes necessary to continuously improve the health and well-being of present and future generations, via both personal and collective decisions and actions. Students with growing proficiency in this space are able to see a future that is sustainable and learn how to navigate the complex path to achieve this. Students, who are often great at seeing problems, are pushed to evolve into solutionists who then have to work through the messy process of crafting solutions. This area also brings action to the learning.

Action in this work includes personal action and collective action. It means adults modeling action for their students. It means leaders modeling action for their staff, and most important, it requires adults to place their areas of advocacy on the table to share with students. Embracing this third standard pushes schools and school leaders to empower students to create and design solutions that truly make a difference in schools, communities, and beyond.

In a slightly different perspective, the Center for Ecoliteracy points to their "fundamental facts of life" that they believe should emerge from educating learners in the areas of Education for Sustainability. These facts include: matter cycles continually throughout the web of life, most of the energy driving the ecological cycles flows from the sun, diversity assures resilience, one species' waste is another species' food, and life did not take over the planet by combat but by networking. Schools have found a number of different entry points to crafting learning on these fundamental facts of life.

For some, this looks like growing vegetable gardens on campus or tending to a colony of bees as a part of a class project. For others, it is about revolutionizing lunch, and making the cafeteria a classroom for learning about nutrition, food waste, and ingredient management. No matter the place of origin, those involved with EfS are pursuing a sustainable society that, as EfS educator Donella Meadows stated, "is far-seeing enough, flexible enough, and wise enough not to undermine either its physical or its social system of support."

QUESTIONS FOR REFLECTION

What areas of current learning in your school are ripe for amplification using the concepts of Education for Sustainability?

What would it look like in your community to have Education for Sustainability as a part of the entire community's mission?

How could Education for Sustainability grow the engagement of the students in your classroom, school, or school district?

RESOURCES

The Cloud Institute for Sustainability Education, http://cloudinstitute. org/

The US Partnership for Education for Sustainable Development, http://k12.uspartnership.org/

The US Partnership for Education for Sustainable Development Standards, https://drive.google.com/file/d/0B96g-ylPKpE5bnVs NFpVdWc0Mkk/edit?usp=sharing

Center for Ecoliteracy, http://www.ecoliteracy.org

The Third Teacher, http://thethirdteacherplus.com/

Shelburne Farms' Sustainable Schools Project, http://www. sustainableschoolsproject.org/

Goleman, Daniel, *Ecoliterate: How Educators Are Cultivating Emotional, Social, and Ecological Intelligence* (Josey Bass, 2012). http://www. ecoliteracy.org/books/ecoliterate-how-educators-are-cultivating-emotional-social-and-ecological-intelligence

SEVEN

Riding the Wave of Technology Integration

We will never be ahead of the wave, maybe the best we can hope for is to be on the crest of the wave. Brad heard these words and knew that his leadership would be tested as he brought the tools needed for technology integration to his students, teachers, and community. Work in schools surrounding technology integration may be the most promising and fastest changing aspect of the educational tapestry.

Every school is scrambling to find the right set of learning tools that maximize the efficiency and effectiveness of instruction. Brad had read about schools fumbling with technology integration, some from moving too slow and others from moving too fast. He was looking for just the right pace to transform learning and give students an opportunity to create, connect, and collaborate at the highest levels.

Technology integration held incredible promise for Brad's school, but the idea of taking the school to a completely different place through the use of technology as opposed to some incremental changes around the edges that looked good in the community would take leadership. Transformational change in schools is rare, and Brad knew that the promise of technology comes deep on the back end of implementation after a whole series of roadblocks and attitudinal barriers are busted. He had read that it takes three years or more to change the culture of use even with the best network and professional development.

Brad knew that his work with technology integration would provide the community with an exciting launch as new computing devices filtered throughout the school, but the real impact on learning would take time, care, and nurturing. Brad wasn't a Luddite. He had grown up surrounded with technological advances, and he used a number of devices to learn throughout his work day, including his desktop in his office, his tablet as he worked throughout the building, and his smartphone beyond the walls of the school. Brad wasn't short on being connected, and he had realized the power of being a connected learner and leader as he built his professional learning network through state organizations, social media, and community partnerships.

He wanted to unleash this flood of learning for his teachers as well. Brad thought that his teachers would embrace new resources and the idea of being connected, but he also wanted the teachers to help the students grow their learning network to extend beyond the classroom. This would be another mind shift for Brad and his staff to work through.

Brad developed three opportunities for his staff to build both their philosophical and practical capacities surrounding engaging students deeply through technology integration. The first opportunity was a chance for a group of staff members to visit schools that were already on the road to success surrounding technology integration. Brad's school wasn't paving a new road, and he wanted to make sure that the school's journey limited the mistakes made by other schools.

During these visits, teachers were able to meet with teachers to talk about the benefits of technology in the classroom and the classroom management techniques necessary for success. They were able to see learning taking place and to talk with students about how learning was different in their classrooms. Brad created space for teachers to wonder and ponder how things would be different in a technology-rich environment. This happened after each school visit so teachers could debrief on what they experienced. Brad used these moments to talk about his vision in a low-key way that wrapped into the conversations as opposed to having his thoughts on top of the conversations.

The teachers asked good questions coming away from these sessions, and Brad was incredibly surprised that the conversation didn't digress into all of the potential problems of technology integration. He knew that facilitating change in education is often about fending off the onslaught of reasons why things can't work. Clearly, his teachers were showing an interest in making this change.

The second opportunity that he provided the teachers was an opportunity to attend one of three "edcamp" events that took place in the region. The edcamp format was a growing force in innovative professional development that allowed the passions and interests of teachers to be at the forefront of the learning. Edcamp events generally take place on Saturdays and are designed to bring together fresh ideas and unleash trapped wisdom into the system. They often have some of the most innovative and progressive educators in the area in attendance.

Brad wanted his teachers to listen and learn from these sessions. The sessions aren't designed as presentations but conversations about best practice. They are ultimately about supporting each other to take positive risks for kids. Edcamps also provide fresh teacher voice, and the folks contributing to the conversation are mostly classroom teachers.

After the first event, where he had three teachers attend, two of them were enthusiastic about going to a second edcamp, and before the week was over, five new teachers asked if they could attend. Before the first semester was complete, half of the staff had attended an edcamp, and more important, they were interested in beginning to do some of their own professional development using some of the engaging best practices that they had seen at edcamp. Teachers were looking to share their ideas, projects, and resources surrounding their early attempts to integrate technology.

The third opportunity that Brad provided for his teachers in this space of transition was the opportunity to work closely with an embedded external technology coach. Even with an increasing amount of wisdom in the system, Brad knew that some of his teachers had learning styles that drew them to working with outside resources.

Many of these teachers had travelled to conferences over the years, and they found great value listening to those teachers and consultants from other spaces. To maximize the value of outside support, Brad decided to bring someone to the building that would spend a total of six days throughout the year working with the teachers. Part of this contract was that the consultant would be available for asynchronous learning opportunities with teachers.

Brad realized that the power of professional development often comes hours or days later when a concept learned runs into context. At that point, the "expert" is gone, and the teachers feel as though they have been abandoned with half-ideas. Brad was convinced that if he was going to bring consultants to the table, they would be folks that would build relationships in his building. Having a consultant in-house also allowed Brad to talk about next steps and the realistic goals that he should be considering for his staff around technology integration for the remainder of the year.

Brad knew that there were a couple of other areas that needed consideration as he asked his staff to bring the power of technology integration through creation, collaboration, and connection to the students. The first was making sure that any increase in devices coming to a campus would be buoyed, not burdened, by the bandwidth and Internet speed on campus. Brad knew of too many initiatives that were doomed from the start by folks not thinking about infrastructure and working from the inside out.

Brad also wanted the staff to take careful consideration about the device or devices that they wanted to bring into the learning space. Brad wanted to be clear that devices are a means to an end, not an end on their own.

Year one of the work to bring more technology integration to the classroom ended with the delivery of a combination of devices for students and teachers. The idea was to give the teachers the summer to explore and prepare for a classroom that would look dramatically different in the fall. Teachers were starting to use common language about how they needed to grow as facilitators and not lead all of the conversations in the classroom. They were talking about continuing to learn and build their network of allies, and they were also talking about creating a safe space for failure and growth for the students and themselves.

Brad believed that the promise of technology integration was so important for his students. He knew that many of the careers that would bring happiness and fulfillment to his students involved having the technical skills that are cultivated through digital learning. Brad would continue to model technology integration practices through his leadership, conversations with parents and the community, and the way that he handled the logistics of the school. Brad wanted his students and staff at the crest of the wave so that they could feel the power and force of technology in their learning, and he knew that achieving this goal would begin through his leadership by example.

QUESTIONS FOR REFLECTION

Does it seem that Brad is finding the right balance with his technology integration initiatives?

How do you provide space and time for teachers to grow as connected educators?

What doors open for students as additional technology is integrated into schools?

EIGHT

Infusing Technology Integration

One of the symbols of modern affluence is access to speedy, reliable broadband and the devices that provide a window into the world of information and learning. Though the rise of inexpensive cellular options have provided an entrance to this world for more and more children in our schools, the reality is that the quality of the access and devices used by the majority of our students in poverty is creating a digital divide that has the potential to stunt their academic growth.

Technology in schools is not an arms race. There is no way to buy your way out of a digital divide. Certainly, money to spend on infrastructure and devices can create the proper glide path for closing the digital divide, but it doesn't guarantee that learning will blossom. Closing the digital divide should be central to the vision of every school that is currently without the technology tools to enhance learning.

A starting place for school leaders looking to build high levels of technology integration in their learning space is the building of common language. Currently, there are community, parent, and teacher mental models about what technology's role in student learning is that are based on these groups' experiences with technology when they were in school. Technology integration has accelerated at such a rate that very little of their mental models are based in current reality. Building a community-wide common language requires a willingness by leaders to exist in the complexity of technology integration.

No longer can the answer to questions from prospective parents about whether a school has technology be about the devices themselves. The response must be layered into a conversation about the learning that emerges from students' creating, connecting, collaborating, and using critical thinking as a part of their dance with their devices.

Technology integration in schools is difficult to measure, and schools and school leaders often resist measuring the difficult parts of learning even though from these difficult spaces great change can emerge. Schools looking to build a common understanding and common language can look to the CASE (Classroom, Access, Skills, Environment) framework developed by BrightBytes. BrightBytes is a company with educational leaders at its core that have developed a robust way to measure technology integration.

Each of these four areas is examined through staff, student, and parent surveys to provide schools with a reliable measure of their effectiveness in closing the digital divide. Choosing these four elements to be the backbone of assessing technology integration came from research surrounding the schools that have created significant impact on learning through technology integration.

Classroom

The final measure of the success of all technology integration efforts lies in the actions of students and teachers in the classroom. How are students using their technology opportunities to analyze and synthesize? How are students showcasing their learning? How are students building future skills for persuasion and storytelling?

Access

The digital divide multiplies when the only access to the world of information for students comes at school. Access to digital tools needs to be continuous for students so that the power of asynchronous learning can be realized. Students need time and space to grow their understanding on the topics and themes presented at school and those that emerge from their personal passions.

Skills

Leaders, teachers, and students in a majority of schools don't have a common understanding about the technology skills necessary for student excellence. It isn't from a lack of trying. The International Society for Technology in Education, or ISTE, has built a set of comprehensive standards around technology integration skills. In addition, there are frameworks like the Technology Integration Matrix from the Florida Center for Instructional Technology and concepts like the Substitution Augmentation Modification Redefinition or SAMR Model.

All of these provide potential language and guidance for schools to use surrounding the skills needed to build proficiency in students and adults. The BrightBytes survey focuses on three areas of skills: foundational, online, and multimedia.

Environment

School culture dictates success in so many ways, and this includes the learning impact that technology integration will make on students. Having school leaders and teacher leaders that support risk taking, failing forward, and space for innovation builds positive energy for technology integration in classrooms. A supportive environment also means creating a culture of service that supports technology that isn't functioning optimally and helping repair, replace, and recycle items in a timely manner.

Once a school has language surrounding what successful technology integration looks like, sounds like, and feels like, the potential power of technology in the hands of students can be realized. In addition, leaders must be ready to open up their classrooms and learning environments by minimizing the technology limits that they place on students. The digital environment that exists outside of the formal learning day has to be quite close to the digital landscape that students have before and after school.

Without this open environment, students don't see school as a place to grow with their technology integration skills, but a place that limits and suppresses the potential engagement in learning that technology brings. This doesn't mean that leaders shouldn't create appropriate limits to balance the use of technology with other excellent learning strategies, but they should continue to examine the boundaries created. Proactive leaders make sure that appropriate use of technology is taught to the students, including the concepts of digital citizenship and digital footprint.

Technology integration exposes classrooms to an incredible wealth of free resources that hold the potential to maximize engagement in the classroom. This includes greater engagement for the introverted student who struggles to participate in classroom discussion or collaborative projects. Technology allows this student to send his or her teacher an e-mail to get questions answered, participate in interactive online classroom discussions, and work with others through collaborative document sharing.

Students who are avid video game players can find greater engagement through technology integration as they are looped back into the learning of the classroom using game theory, gamification, and educational games that go to the heart of the standards being taught in the classroom. In addition, the ideas of competency-based learning, that break learning into discrete parts, can play a role in recapturing some learners that are overwhelmed by the learning path of the majority.

Technology integration allows for heightened engagement for all students as more classrooms provide students with opportunities to showcase their learning and creativity using digital tools. Students will work hours and hours on multiple drafts to produce excellent work when technology is infused into the process. Examples of this can be seen in student blogs, video production, and digital storytelling opportunities that fill the electronic spaces of schools involved with technology integration.

Technology integration also allows students to grow savvier in their technology consumption. Students are bombarded with thousands of photos and videos each day, and part of the learning process on how to produce quality digital pieces is combing through and curating the content being viewed for quality examples to emulate. School leaders want their students to be both quality consumers and producers in this nonstop digital space.

Technology will never replace great teaching. Teachers are able to ask not only the first question, but the second question that is based on looking a student in the eye, seeing their body language, and knowing their history. Great teachers are embracing the power of technology integration as they recognize the complexity of today's teaching and the need for more personal learning that requires no tools be left unused. Every piece of technology that students are using today will be the worst technology that they have in their lifetime, but this doesn't mean that schools shouldn't be looking to close the digital divide and maximize engagement through the balanced integration of technology tools and applications that shower today's educational space.

QUESTIONS FOR REFLECTION

What is the right balance for schools when it comes to technology integration?

How can we best judge engagement in our students surrounding technology integration?

In what ways can classrooms, schools, and districts amplify the creating, connecting, and collaborating happening for kids through technology integration?

RESOURCES

Clarity from BrightBytes, www.brightbytes.net
edcampSTL—A Piece of the Unconference Movement, www.edcampstl.wikispaces.com
International Society for Technology in Education (ISTE), www.iste.org
ISTE Standards, www.iste.org/standards
Consortium for Social Networking (CoSN), http://www.cosn.org/

NINE

Throwing Away the Box

The students learning at Brad's school were excited about the experiences that took place outside and in the community. It gave them something to look forward to, a reason to focus on their learning, and a way for their strengths to shine. A gap though had grown between these large experiences and the daily learning being planned by Brad's teachers. It wasn't that the instruction was subpar, but it wasn't superb either. Brad knew that there was a need to build day-to-day programming that could also maximize engagement. He began looking for ways to make each day in his classrooms as exciting for students as the expeditionary learning opportunities.

Inspiration for this next phase of leadership came to Brad when he was having dinner with a friend who was a kindergarten teacher. She was talking about a town in Italy that was known for its teaching practices that allowed students to construct their learning based on their passions. They would then build knowledge around those interests, and use their learning space as inspiration for growth. She said that Reggio Emilia, Italy, has been steeped in this tradition of learning for years, and she was trying some of these new ideas in her classroom.

Brad's friend, Maria, talked for almost an hour about her students' excitement surrounding their most recent project. They were learning about squirrels, and the class had built a place for the animals to play as well as designed a way to assist them in their leaps from the tree to the fence. Her students were coming to school every Monday ready to report about the behavior of the squirrels in their neighborhood.

Maria said that the books, games, and math lessons in her class were being built around this learning, and she loved the extra time outside doing genuine observation of the neighborhood. This conversation had the wheels spinning for Brad. Though he knew that he couldn't replicate the exact model that Maria and the village in Northern Italy had in place, he did believe that he was on to something.

Passion-based learning or project-based learning had cycled through Brad's learning as a student in middle school, his graduate work, and as an assistant principal at a former school. It was an idea that always felt like the right way to do education. It would provide students with an opportunity to build real solutions for real problems while weaving a variety of other learning into the process.

He recognized that his primary attraction to project-based learning was that it was an opportunity to make school feel like life as opposed to school feeling like it was just preparation for life. Brad started to explore the possibility of bringing project-based learning to his staff by creating a challenge for them around their professional development for the year.

At the start of the year, he outlined a scenario that would shape the professional development for the year. It was a context that provided meaning, purpose, and engagement for the adult learning that would take place throughout the year. Brad talked with the staff about the power of releasing trapped wisdom into the system, and how they had a responsibility to support learning not only in their classrooms and their schools, but within education in general.

To do this, groups of teachers were challenged to build a suite of professional development activities that would support this effort. Teachers began to look for ways to share their best lessons. They posted them on lesson plan sharing sites, on Twitter, and used their professional networks to share their work. A number of teachers had started their own repositories in Wikispaces and Google Sites that they feverishly shared with other teachers in their subject areas and beyond.

The second part of the challenge that Brad posed was for each of his teachers to look for others that teach their subject at a very high level and begin to learn from them. He wanted teachers to reach out to folks that were excelling in the craft of teaching and begin a conversation that would allow for growth and learning. Twice during the year, Brad created space for teachers to share about this process internally. Teachers were encouraged to reflect on the process of sharing, and then they worked as a staff to think about next steps, missteps, and steps in the right direction.

This work with teachers brought new energy to their learning, and many teachers saw value in bringing this type of learning to students. One team of teachers started talking about a challenge that would bring students closer to their community. It was a challenge to have students help raise neighborhood awareness about daily water usage. Through their studies in science, the students knew that awareness alone could bring a reduction in the use of potable water for usages such as watering lawns, washing cars, and running outside water features.

The teachers seized on this area of interest that the students expressed to build additional studies on water. They had students working on finding documents and informational materials that could persuade neighbors to conserve their water use. Other students were collecting and analyzing data based on observations during school hours and in the evening on water use throughout the community. Students also were researching other communities that had taken up this cause and were building their knowledge around the lessons learned in those communities.

Throughout this process, which was about three weeks in total, students were journaling, blogging, photographing, and documenting their learning. Brad noticed that the three-week project took a toll on his teachers. They were exhausted. The amount of moving parts in this type of learning was hard to control for teachers, but it was even harder for them to realize the need to relinquish control in this space.

Some teachers worried about test scores and time away from "real learning," but energy from the students was also overwhelming as the teachers weren't used to students being so intense concerning their learning. Brad was second-guessing whether asking his teachers to attempt to build a continuous project-based environment was just too much. Had he pushed them to a breaking point? It would certainly be easier to revert back. All weekend Brad worried about the next steps; then one of his teachers called him on Sunday.

Mrs. Evans was a veteran teacher. She had been teaching for fifteen years in the same classroom, and she was the school's teacher of the year just five years earlier. When she called Brad, she apologized for interrupting his weekend, but she needed to tell him thank you. She said that the project around water awareness had changed her as a teacher. She had always wanted to see her students working in a way that could serve the community, but she never felt supported from her team or by the building leadership to take the leap.

She talked about how tired that she was all weekend, but she also told Brad stories of the the excitement her students had about the project; many had never gotten excited about learning in the past. She wasn't sure what the next project-based learning experience would be, but she was making a commitment to doing one project each quarter. Brad breathed a sigh of relief. He knew now that he was on the right track.

When Brad returned on Monday, he met with one of his social studies teachers, Doug, who was struggling with how to work with his team. The teacher was struggling because he felt like his philosophy was so different from that of his colleagues. He was the first teacher to embrace the experiential learning work, but he couldn't convince his team to dive into this project-based learning journey.

Brad encouraged Doug to bunker down a bit and begin to build a unit in his classroom that supported the tenants of project-based learning. Both Doug and Brad knew that working independently in a project-based learning environment was much more difficult, but Brad had a hunch

that this teacher and the energy of the students coming out of his classroom would spark some additional interest.

Doug was one of Brad's teachers who was willing to take a risk as
long as he knew that there could be a payoff for kids. He had transferred
to Brad's school after spending the previous ten years of his career in a
school with much higher scores and an easier environment in which to
teach. He made the shift to Brad's school because he had a desire to
"truly make an impact on kids that needed a good teacher." Doug was
glad that Brad was bringing a new sense of energy and a fresh level of
trust. It fed into his desire to change his small portion of the world.

Doug was beginning a unit on the causes of the Civil War, and he
stared at a pile of worksheets and projects that he had been using for five
or six years. He found a box, dropped the entire pile inside, and sealed it
with tape. He told himself that if everything for the next three weeks
went completely pear-shaped then he would open the box, but if not, he
would throw the box away for good.

Doug talked to a few teachers in other schools that were more sea-
soned in project-based learning as he didn't want to make the same mistakes. They shared openly about their experiences. They encouraged him
to have some clear guiding questions, but to remain open to questions
generated by students as they often turned out to be the most powerful
places of exploration.

The teachers talked about the difficulty in building the tight/loose
mentality that it takes to be successful in this space, and they warned
Doug that he would get a lot more wrong than right in his first project.
They also talked about the importance of building structures throughout
the process to scaffold the project. This would help to meet the needs of
all students, especially those that weren't strong in the area of internal
motivation.

Doug was ready to fail forward, and he took some time to design his
Civil War unit based on guiding questions that had no specific answers.
He developed a menu of opportunities for kids to showcase their learning that provided student choice and student voice. He built a set of
learning experiences that brought together local experts, community resources, and a fresh set of video resources that supported the primary
documents that he was already using. Activities in this project had students examining how their community would have been affected if the
Civil War had ended differently.

Doug pushed the students past the idea of focusing just on the outcomes of the war. He had students looking at maps from local spaces that
were impacted by the war, and by using Google Maps, they were able to
identify a cemetery with Civil War graves.

The class travelled there and met a local historian who discussed the
stories of the past surrounding the space in which the students were
standing. To bring the project together, the students combined their

learning into a Google Site. Developing the website supported the learning of page design as well as the importance of accuracy in reporting to maintain credibility with a public audience. Doug worked hard, but the students worked harder. In the end, Doug knew that he wasn't going back to his box. He was moving forward with new energy and a set of students that were ready for their next challenge.

QUESTIONS FOR REFLECTION

How could you support a teacher that wanted to put it all "in a box"?

What areas of a school improvement plan could be shaped as project-based learning for adults?

What elements of project-based learning are ripe for growth in your learning spaces?

TEN

Beyond the Volcano

The concept of students doing projects for school is a piece of the personal history for most parents around the world. This often included last-minute runs to the store for supplies for creating a volcano, building a model of a fort, or designing a poster board of the solar system. Projects have been a rite of passage for parents for years. One of the most famous projects, the science fair project, attempts to bring the beauty of the scientific method into practice for students young and old, but mostly it creates a construction and art project for parents with little learning for students.

These projects, that are remembered as a part of family lore, create stress, push parents into the center of the learning, and struggle to meet the claim that the time spent was worth the learning that took place. Reconstructing this mental model of "school projects" has been central to the mission of the advocates of project-based learning. Project-based learning moves away from the folly of the projects of the past and instead creates rich learning spaces that engage students deeply in meaningful, rigorous learning.

One of the biggest advocates for excellent project-based learning is the Buck Institute for Education. This organization has the mission of improving teaching and learning throughout the world by creating and disseminating products, practices, and knowledge for effective project-based learning (PBL). The Buck Institute for Education provides both free and paid resources that can launch schools into a stronger place around project-based learning. Following the Buck Institute for Education's "essential elements" of project-based learning allows for meaningful outcomes for students as they make connections between previous and future learning.

The first essential element is that the project is focused on significant content that is deeply embedded in the standards-based curriculum of the school. The knock on many of the historic classroom projects is that they were shallow in content and a tangent to the core of learning. Today's project-based learning begins by having the project emerge from the key concepts at the heart of an academic subject. This means that model fort of the War of 1812 may be a fun project, but this isn't the core learning on this topic.

The focus from the beginning must be on significant pieces of the learning journey. It is also key that students have an opportunity to create, connect, and collaborate. These are the skills that students need hours and hours to practice because in these moments of engaged practice come high levels of perseverance, grit, and determination.

Project-based learning takes time. There is no way around the fact that doing this type of learning requires a time commitment by teachers and learners. The pressure of coverage has to be removed from the teachers for project-based learning to be a success. It requires that in-depth inquiry is occurring. This looks like students asking questions, using a variety of resources, and developing answers. It means spending time in conversation with peers, adults, and learning mentors outside of the classroom. It also means inquiry that is open to exploration but is focused on the driving questions of the project.

These driving questions should be ones without an obvious answer that create space for students to examine concepts and ideas from a variety of angles. For schools that have worked with the Understanding by Design framework for curriculum development, the driving questions of project-based learning are siblings to the enduring understandings and essential questions of that framework. It is essential that the leadership supporting project-based learning carve out the time needed to have in-depth professional conversations about the just right language for the project's driving questions.

It is also important that the driving questions are broad and focused, interesting and engaging, and relevant and weighty. One of the early pitfalls to project-based learning is not spending enough time in this space. Because without the right foundational questions, the life is eventually zapped out of the project.

Imagine being at a concert and the band's first two songs are ones that they have never played before or are the slowest ones in their repertoire; the band would fail to launch the needed energy for an excellent concert. This idea can be transferred to project-based learning.

The entry event, another of the essential elements, is the key hook to engage students in the learning for the project. This can be a new experience beyond the school walls, a compelling speaker, or an examination of documents and data that elicits emotion. There are a variety of options based on the audience and the location, but this learning moment or entry event can be a tipping point for the creation of a memorable project-based learning experience.

Following the entry event, lead learners should return to the core engagement practices including bringing student choice and student voice to the center of the learning. This means having learning paths for students that vary and tap into areas of student passion. Project-based learning also finds excellence when there is time for iteration that includes peer review and public comment. Doing so allows students to continue to return to the same piece of work following self-reflection and peer feedback.

Students also need time to reflect and celebrate at the end of the project. This cements learning and promotes a desire to learn in a project-based learning environment in the future. Finally, excellence emerges in PBL when the teacher isn't the last arbiter of excellence, and the learning isn't trapped in the classroom. Best practice allows for a public audience to fill the project-based learning spaces that are being created.

Classrooms, schools, and networks of schools such as the New Tech Network are finding that using project-based learning and its essential elements allows for a natural curiosity for learning to emerge. The emergence occurs because the project is central to the learning throughout the unit as opposed to being at the end of the unit used to only assess learning.

After school leaders spend time developing their school's common language surrounding excellent, engaging project design, it is essential to spend time having conversations with teachers, parents, and students around how to assess the excellence that comes from project-based learning. Unlike traditional forms of assessing learning, there is a complexity that comes with these engaging units of study.

One attempt at excellent assessment of PBL comes from the work of schools in the New Tech Network that have modified the work of Adria Steinberg's 6 A's. The 6 A's, described in detail in the book *Real Learning, Real Work,* provide language and probing questions to examine and reflect on the effectiveness of a project. The 6 A's are authenticity, academic rigor, applied learning, active exploration, adult connections, and assessment practices.

Authentic projects simulate real-world adult problem solving and create a natural desire for students to lean in for further exploration. Ideally this means the work that the students are doing will actually be used by a group or organization outside of the school to further their mission or work. Authenticity also breeds a sense of pride in students as they see great social value and personal value in their work.

Having academic rigor seems commonsensical for planning excellent project-based learning, but this is an area that is often overlooked and underreflected upon in the planning process at many schools first implementing project-based learning. Ideas for projects that engage students often emerge easily, but being able to nest that project into local, state, or national standards is an artful dance for educators. In addition to creating the conditions for rigorous academic work, excellent PBL will also foster learning habits such as persistence, examining multiple viewpoints, and careful curation of evidence.

Project-based learning continues to showcase the fact that leading a classroom is about facilitating the learning as opposed to the teacher providing all of the information for students. PBL contains tenets of constructivism and discovery-based learning as the acquisition of new knowledge and skills in this learning environment often evolves more naturally as students unwrap the layers of the driving questions.

Along with this, there is also a need for new skills, concepts, and ideas to be interwoven into the learning by a master teacher. Once the right balance is struck from these two angles of learning, students can mold and shape their learning using the organization and management skills embedded in PBL such as building a work plan, collaborating and communicating with teammates, meeting deadlines, and allowing individual strengths in the group to shine.

In the active exploration space of PBL, learners are using skills like observing and interviewing, researching online for primary sources and other quality information, and conducting experiments and testing hypotheses. Excellent PBL also tends to have peer review, conferencing, and short-cycle prototyping, which adds to student engagement.

The final two elements of the 6 A's allow for an authentic audience to play a deep role in project-based learning. It showcases the "real" nature of the learning by surrounding the learners with additional experts that can support the unit of study. This includes adults and mentors from the community and beyond. Often this means using videoconferencing and other electronic connections to enrich the learning.

In the best scenarios, students have the opportunity to work alongside adult mentors that are working on the same or similar projects as a part of their career. This can also include creating multiple paths for students to showcase their learning through public presentations, portfolios, and perhaps video and audio pieces to enhance a student's digital footprint.

Project-based learning provides an excellent opportunity for schools to empower students. Leaders, teacher leaders, and others looking to infuse this instructional strategy into their learning ecosystem in a sustainable way should also consider using the essential elements and the 6 A's of project-based learning in the organizational management of the school in areas such as master scheduling, intervention development, and technology integration initiatives. This can provide the modeling necessary for the positive risk-taking needed by teachers to have successful project-based learning.

QUESTIONS FOR REFLECTION

How are you using the concepts in the 6 A's to maximize engagement for students?

Is there a single unit of study in your classroom that is ripe for transition to project-based learning?

What driving questions are naturally emanating from your school and community?

RESOURCES

Buck Institute for Education, http://www.bie.org/tools/freebies
Edutopia, http://www.edutopia.org/project-based-learning
Steinberg, Adria, *Real Learning, Real Work: School-to-Work as High School Reform* (Routledge, 1997).
New Tech Network, http://www.newtechnetwork.org/
The Project Approach, http://www.projectapproach.org/

ELEVEN

Building Connected Conversations through Systems Thinking

Brad was concerned that the learning of his students was compartmentalized, too subject specific, and that students were struggling to see how the sciences and humanities intersected. He had definitely seen an increase in the interest in learning because of the work being done at the school, but he longed for students to go deeper. During this time of reflection surrounding the growth of his school, Brad was having a weekend coffee with a couple of friends who worked in banking in Chicago. They mentioned how hard it was for many of the bankers in their organization to understand and think in a systematic way about how their actions impacted the greater society.

They mentioned that so many of their colleagues were trapped by the numbers in front of them that they failed to allow the human element to enter into their decision making. Many of the senior managers worried that the next generation of senior leadership that they were grooming wouldn't possess the skills needed to see the big picture or have the tools to think in systems.

They believed that graduate schools were producing specialists without these skills, and they even worried that colleges and high schools were perpetuating the idea that career readiness is about getting students completely immersed in specialized skills needed for careers as opposed to creating thinkers, learners, and communicators who can explain complex concepts to a variety of audiences.

This conclusion led the senior management team to take ten managers on a week-long quest to build capacity in systems thinking. Brad thought the logic that the senior management of the bank had applied to this situation could be applied to his school as well. He wanted to build capacity in his teachers, and systems thinking may allow this to happen.

It would allow the school a better chance to build a different type of student, a student that saw connections, acted with deep empathy, and took actions that leveraged change and minimized unintended negative consequences.

Brad left that small Chicago coffeehouse with a piece of wisdom from an unlikely source. From there, he spent some time digging deeply into the concept of systems thinking. One conclusion that emerged for Brad was that systems thinking had the potential to allow the learning of his students to go much deeper. He also saw great potential in having more of the academic conversations evolve into social emotional growth for his students as systems thinking would allow for whole, big picture, empathetic thinking.

As students started to look at things from new perspectives, the conversations were rich, and the students were truly feeling the discomfort of breaking away from their inherited mental models to mental models that they were now creating on their own. Mental models lie at the heart of all systems, but they aren't obvious in the beginning. It takes a learning journey through the events, assumptions, and beliefs to get to the core of why thinking and actions happen. Brad's young thinkers were working very hard to be in this space.

Prior to the success that was being realized by the students, Brad had brought systems thinking to his staff. He was careful to bring these ideas and resources to his staff in context; systems thinking can be one of those abstract adult learning concepts that gets buried by the day-to-day needs. Brad instead posed a challenge. He asked his staff what type of school would best create the student that the world needs to solve the toughest of problems. He pushed them to think about building an ecosystem that would allow their kids to be the leaders needed to change the world.

This was big thinking, and many of the teachers laughed at the hyperbole, but he was asking them to dig beyond a school that was just getting better to a school that would be a model for others and unique in its mission. He knew that to get to that type of thinking his staff would need to work with three or four of the structures of systems thinking.

He used these bimonthly conversations to introduce behavior over time graphs (BOTG), a construct to bring a visual narrative to the behavior of a situation over time. Teachers used these graphs to look at how students behave from the beginning of the year until the end; they also used BOTG to discuss how teacher behavior toward learning was shaped over the course of a year and over the course of a career.

They looked at how the acceptance of things such as technology integration, project-based learning, and Education for Sustainability occurred in the larger community. They looked at how much time was spent directly preparing for tests over the course of the year. All of these BOTGs gave rise to rich conversations, and they prepared the teachers for a second phase of conversation.

Brad next had teachers place each of the behavior over time graphs around a circle for the purpose of talking about how they connected. He wanted to push his teachers past the events themselves into a space that allowed them to see how each of these "separate" behaviors either created a reinforcing loop where one item amplifies and feeds the next item, which in turn reinforces the first, or whether the relationship creates a balancing loop that allows the two events to exist in a more symbiotic relationship.

Some of the answers to these questions weren't obvious to the staff, and they wrestled with how many of the behaviors and actions of the system supported each other or negatively impacted the work that was being done. These conversations often left more questions than answers, but it was clear that, as the staff worked through some of these structures surrounding systems thinking, they were able to see how many of the activities that they were using to learn themselves could spark engagement for kids in their classrooms.

The final thing that Brad introduced to his teachers were the habits of a systems thinker. These habits provided some additional common language for the staff surrounding systems thinking, and they allowed staff and eventually students to begin to name their thinking and actions throughout the learning day. The habits include the idea that a systems thinker (1) recognizes that a system's structure generates its behavior, (2) considers an issue fully and resists the urge to come to a quick conclusion, and (3) understands a system's structure to identify possible leverage actions.

It was amazing to watch many of the staff members grasp the concepts of systems thinking. Brad saw a breath of fresh air come over many of them as they found a new way to approach old material. He saw teachers excited about bringing this language into their classrooms to help students access materials at a new level.

The first teachers to use systems thinking in the classroom were his science teachers. They saw easy connections to their work around cycles, ecosystems, and our interconnected planet. Brad's science teachers used the tools and common language to promote some of the environmental education mission as well as to connect students to the behavior of the planet and people over time. Brad's social studies teachers also saw an opening to use systems thinking in their learning. They were able to look at historical events and the reasons for those events in a more systematic and logical way. They were able to chart behavior over time and connect the issues surrounding wars and conflicts in a more deep and meaningful way. The best part for the social studies teachers was that they already had students with a base vocabulary on systems thinking that had been taught in the science classrooms.

About a semester later, both the language arts and math teachers were still looking for ways to move the tools of systems thinking into their learning spaces in an authentic way. Brad worked with them to find real moments in their curriculum where these tools could bolster their conversations. In language arts, students talked about characters' behavior over time and with some novels how the multifaceted plot was connected using a connection circle.

In math, the teachers used the ladder of inference, another of the systems thinking tools, to dig into their mental models about math and explore the concepts that students were born without math skills and that they hated math. These two areas were often mental blocks for Brad's students in math, and he was glad that they weren't avoiding these tough conversations. Systems thinking was growing. Students were growing, and deeper, more connected conversations were becoming the norm within the learning spaces of Brad's school.

QUESTIONS FOR REFLECTIONS

Do the teachers and students in your learning space see and learn in systems? How could this develop more deeply?

How do you as a leader find new ideas outside of education that you can use to make schools better?

Do you possess the habits of a systems thinker? How could you grow your understanding in this arena of learning?

TWELVE

Seeing in Systems

The world makes sense in systems and patterns. It is only when moments and experiences are connected into an already established schema that new growth, refinements to understanding, and fresh perspectives can emerge in our learning. Systems surround life, and the learning that comes from thinking in systems is an essential area of growth for the students living in this global community. When students see the connections between life and school in their daily learning opportunities, there is a natural heightening of engagement. The classic student question of "why are we doing this?" is minimized as systems thinking grows, and the focus returns to the work at hand.

The Waters Foundation has built capacity in the area of systems thinking in teachers and students throughout the United States and beyond over the course of almost two decades. Their primary focus has been on the visual structures of systems thinking, including the ladder of inference, behavior over time graphs, stock/flow diagrams, the iceberg visual, and causal loop diagrams. According to the Waters Foundation, these tools help students and educators collect, analyze, synthesize, and communicate their thoughts about systems. In addition to these visual structures, the Waters Foundation promotes students having the opportunity to grow as systems thinkers by also spending time building the habits of a systems thinker.

The thirteen habits of a systems thinker provide students with common language to explain why and how the world around them feels different because of systems thinking. These habits are: seeks to understand the big picture; observes how elements within systems change over time, generating patterns and trends; recognizes that a system's structure generates its behavior; identifies the circular nature of complex cause and effect relationships; changes perspectives to increase understanding; surfaces and tests assumptions; considers an issue fully and resists the urge to come to a quick conclusion; considers how mental models affect current reality and the future; uses understanding of system structure to identify possible leverage actions; considers both short- and long-term consequences of actions; finds where unintended consequences emerge; recognizes the impact of time delays when exploring cause and effect relationships; and checks results and changes action if needed.

Students who have this language are engaged. They tend to lean into additional classroom discussion, bring coherence to their thoughts in writing, and build more mature relationships with their teachers and fellow classmates.

The beauty of the visual structures is that they can be used in all subject areas as well as to connect the work across subject areas. One structure, the behavior over time graph (BOTG), provides a way to create a narrative about an occurrence. Students have used BOTGs in social studies to discuss the timeline of the Civil War as it related to the strength of the Confederacy and to describe the rise of patriotism following the events of 9/11.

In science, BOTGs can be used to describe the natural phenomena in school gardens or how water works its way through a watershed over time. In literature, BOTGs can be used to describe the behavior of characters over time in a story. In all of these cases, students are making sense of their work through a simple graphing activity.

The students are putting words and ideas into a visual format that cements the deeper themes of the learning. BOTGs are an observational way to graph behavior that promotes analysis without getting trapped in the numbers. As students grow to use and understand this tool, they are able to discuss in-depth, complex issues using a more robust vocabulary.

This builds energy to the learning spaces, rich conversation, and empowered students. Students on the journey to becoming systems thinkers can rarely leave this learning at school. Students begin to see levers of change at home, including better ways to organize the kitchen, how to deal with sharing technology devices, and methods for solving the issues with a noisy neighbor.

Other visual strategies associated with systems thinking include causal loop diagrams and connection circles that help students to make connections between the elements of a system. Often students involved with systems thinking bring a new vocabulary into their personal lives to explain the areas that they struggle to control. Though the words alone don't bring solace to some of the stress levers in their ecosystem, the words do provide a way to describe, understand, and normalize these experiences. Systems thinking can help reduce the acute stress issues that limit our students from engaging more fully in their work.

Another powerful strategy is the ladder of inference. One teacher who uses the ladder of inference describes it as a way to surface more of the reasoning behind moments in life that we struggle to explain. This way of thinking calls for students and learners to look beyond the events of the day to the patterns that exist between the events and to the systems that surround these patterns. This way of thinking allows for students to have additional control and choice in how school and life impacts them. Students that work deeply into this model move into a place of understanding about how their mental models and beliefs impact everything in their lives including routines, habits, and decisions.

When students have a greater understanding of these visual structures, they tend to find greater uses for the habits of a systems thinker. These thirteen habits, though simple on the surface, represent a journey of learning and growth that is rarely actualized. Each of these habits can be practiced across the curriculum, in any unit, throughout the year. These habits also promote a growth mindset. Students thinking in systems see that their brain is a muscle and is ready to grow strong with hard work and excellent scholarship. The students are also ready to have a skeleton in which to hang their learning and a lens to help curate the flood of information. Systems thinking can serve as this glue.

The work of systems thinking in schools has its roots in organizational management and learning. The book *The Fifth Discipline* by Peter Senge describes how organizations can and should continue to grow as a healthy place of learning for all of its members. In order to impact change in education circles, Senge transitioned this knowledge to the education space, and his findings were synthesized in the book *Schools That Learn*. This book holds much of the foundational wisdom surrounding systems thinking in K–12 education. To support those growing with systems thinking in schools, Senge and others have built a loose network of schools that collaborate and grow together.

The Society for Organizational Learning Education Partnership (SoLEd) serves this role for school districts around the country that see great value in promoting systems thinking. The partnership has a vision to "inspire and equip students, their schools, and their communities to learn together in creating a just, sustainable, and vibrant future."

The respect for the interconnected nature of learning brought SoLEd to build its work around four pillars: systems thinking, Education for Sustainability, youth leadership, and organizational learning. Each of these pillars contains necessary work for schools of excellence. They are interconnected and work as a system to build a culture of learning and engagement that is essential for deep learning by all students.

Schools embracing these foundational practices have brought new levels of energy and excitement to their learning space. This energy and excitement comes over time as the adult understanding and capacity to implement these strategies take root. When beginning this journey, the adult learning track and the student learning track should run in parallel so both groups learn can symbiotically. It is important to also give adults safe spaces to practice this work. Faculty meetings, summer retreats, and other meetings are opportunities to begin having teachers look at schools and/or school districts as systems to show how the parts are interdependent and require strategic decisions to leverage change.

This growing understanding of interdependence will also breed the unintended consequences of self-awareness in an organization, allowing members to see the need to break from their silo into a more open, transparent space that releases trapped wisdom into the system. Adults as systems thinkers can ignite an organization. Students as systems thinkers can change an entire community.

Students want to feel that the power of change is within their reach. They want a way to frame life in their own words with their own voice so that they feel that they are choosing the journey in front of them as opposed to having it dictated to them. Systems thinking is a capacity building structure for this level of empowerment and engagement in schools.

QUESTIONS FOR REFLECTION

What habits of a systems thinker do you see as essential for students and adults?

How do the visual structures of systems thinking have the potential to facilitate change in your organization?

What curricular connections would you like to tie together for greater understanding in your students, teachers, or community?

RESOURCES

Waters Foundation, http://watersfoundation.org/systems-thinking/overview/

Schools That Learn by Peter Senge, http://schoolsthatlearn.com/

Society for Organizational Learning Education Partnership, http://soledpartnership.org/resources/

THIRTEEN

The Power of Story

Incredible things were happening at Brad's school. He was experiencing a new sense of energy in students, teachers, and parents. He was also truly enjoying the hard work that goes with leadership. He was working harder, but feeling better. The grind that is an essential part of school leadership was now filled with moments of innovation, great conversations, and students involved with projects in which they were passionate. Brad knew that he had to seize this energy, and begin to make sure that the incredible work that was being done throughout the school was being archived, celebrated, and shared throughout the community.

Brad had always believed in the power of story; he knew that it was important to begin to craft the narrative of the learning at the school. Schools throughout his community were feeling a backlash from news stories about their poor test scores, their handling of finances, and their decaying facilities for learning. Each of these stories was building a boat anchor around the possibility that greater innovation would be possible for these schools.

Brad knew that if the community at large could see or hear the work happening at his school that he would create some space for his teachers to remain true to the mission and initiatives of the school. In addition, Brad thought that helping his students learn the art of storytelling would be a lifelong skill that would transfer from career to career and from passion to passion.

Brad was looking for a way for both student voice and excellent student work to come to the forefront. He examined a number of tools and options before stepping forward with a twofold concept for capturing the stories of his school. The first would be an electronic portfolio for each of his students that captured video, text, and artifacts of student learning. Students would use the electronic portfolio to capture the best examples of their learning, and it would also provide a place for student reflection. The school would use artifacts to communicate with parents, the community, and beyond.

The second phase for Brad would be having each student build a capstone video that showcased a piece of how they had grown in their thinking, interest or passion, and/or strength over their time at the school. This digital story would serve as a showcase of their technology integration skills, ability to craft a compelling narrative, and it would build a strong visual representation of their story.

Rolling out the electronic portfolio required an intense amount of communication by Brad. He worked with a variety of teacher groups, including a visioning committee, each of his academic teams, his teachers that taught students outside of the core subjects, and a final polishing and design group. In typical Brad style, he accelerated the timeline to complete the e-portfolio because he couldn't imagine another student leaving his school without this experience. It was designed from the outset to be a public document with private spaces. The teachers and students involved with the design conversations wanted the electronic portfolio to be both a showcase and a sandbox.

They saw a need for portfolio quality work to be front and center coupled with a space for reflection. They also believed that the learning process never ends, so the need to have a space for continuous growth and progress was also valuable. Brad worked with the teachers to develop the right concepts to showcase in the electronic portfolio. In the beginning, there was talk about each subject area having a space, but the collective wisdom of the teacher team was that there were important places of interconnection that now existed in the school, and they wanted that way of thinking to be represented in the e-portfolio as well.

This thinking led the design team to build spaces that fed into this philosophy. Students were asked to add excellent work to sections on personal growth over time, interdisciplinary project work, examples of media (books, video, audio, etc.) that had helped them grow as scholars, and ways that they had demonstrated creativity and innovation.

Once the vision of the project intersected with the design, it was time for students to interact with the e-portfolio. A pilot team of students entered information, and they discussed the bumps and friction of the new system. The issues for the students about the prototype were mostly surrounding the limitations that they had in personalizing the space and how some items didn't drop easily into the system.

The teacher team had decided to keep the public space of the e-portfolio heavily branded with the colors of the school as many of these would be shared with a public audience and serve a larger purpose than student private reflection spaces. It became a teachable moment for Brad and his staff as they talked about a digital footprint with the students, first impressions, and design.

Brad continued to see growth in the quality of the final products that students were posting as well as how students were using their private space in the e-portfolio to store personal ideas, projects, and learning beyond the school day. Brad's district decided to use this type of portfolio district-wide, and he was excited to be receiving students in the future that had experience adding items to the e-portfolio so that they can hit the ground running.

A capstone video that allowed students to showcase their growth in storytelling and engage a broader audience was the second phase. This project was designed to have students build a digital story that spoke to their growth over time. Students were highly engaged throughout the project because they were able to tell their story and share a window into their lives. Each year the best videos would be shown on graduation night with the others displayed on the school's YouTube channel. Some of the best videos explored topics such as depression and grief. Others dealt with maturing from being a young girl into a leader and working hard in the weight room to control anger.

In these five-minute videos, he saw raw emotion, and a set of young emerging voices. These students now had a sense that story would play a role in their careers and in changing the world. Students began to see that writing for a cause stirred emotion and persuaded others to action. In the second and third year of this work, the teachers were able to manage the project with greater ease, including scaffolding for those that needed it, shortening the time from start to finish without losing quality, and maximizing the deep learning aspects of the project.

The quality of the student work went up each year as they used excellent exemplars from the previous years to model their quest for quality. Students used a variety of technology tools that allowed for additional video and audio editing and effects to enhance their projects. They used quality video cameras and lighting, and sound equipment that Brad had added for the projects. Students were now spending time on weekends gathering fresh photos and video from home.

They were mining albums and DVDs for moments of their youth that shaped their story. Each of these technology tools enhanced the quality of the projects, but the teachers were also focused on keeping the core of these projects based on writing excellent narrative.

Students labored over each draft to get it just right. They wanted the audio to lie perfect over top of their visuals. They wanted each word to pop. The students crafted a tone that brought the vivid nature of the pictures to life. They realized that writing was the work of craftsmen, and they felt the power of the hard work.

This capstone project became a rite of passage for students. They wanted their story to be heard and celebrated. Brad used many of these projects to showcase the learning that had taken place to the community and beyond. Each story provided a counternarrative to those voices that focused only on test scores to judge schools. He was able to showcase for the community in a real way that the skills of reading, writing, creating, and producing were valuable, and each had an essential place in the common mission of the school.

QUESTIONS FOR REFLECTION

Are you the storyteller-in-chief of your classroom, school, or district?

Which students in your schools do you see getting the biggest benefit from the infusion of story into the classroom?

Does Brad take the right steps surrounding e-portfolios? What would you have done differently?

FOURTEEN

Engaging Learners through Story

Storytelling is the most natural of human conditions. It is how humans make sense of experiences, craft a narrative about fulfilled and unfulfilled dreams, share that which is unseen and unnoticed by others, and persuade others to believe and value what they do. Story is how we avoid making the same mistakes as those who have come before us, and story is how we celebrate the memories of our childhood, family, and community. Though storytelling is the most natural of human conditions that engages both head and heart, schools struggle to use the power of story to bolster the engagement of students.

Story brings comfort, and story brings hope. All story is personal and unique, and all story is universal. This is one of the many messages that comes from the book *Storycatcher* by Christina Baldwin as she describes how as story intensifies in spaces, connection is realized. Learners begin to recognize the unique nature of those surrounding them and how their stories weave together. This bond grows empathy and the relationships between students. It brings energy to classrooms, schools, and school districts.

Story also provides the energy to engage in the hard work necessary for learning. It grows learners to be good citizens in their community and beyond. Story and the power of story deserve a place at the table of learning as schools attempt to balance their instruction and explore deeper ways of learning. Story surrounds life. Children and adults are surrounded by the persuasive power of stories on television, in video, and at the mall. Story is on billboards. Story is in every photo, both taken and untaken. Story is a flood in the rainstorm of life.

Figuring out how to curate and make sense of this flood of information is a very difficult task for both adults and students. Most humans become overwhelmed by information, facts, and the story that passes them each day. They are grabbing pieces, ignoring others, and trying to make sense of all the story that surrounds them. Building the visual literacy necessary in students is a key skill that both slows the torrent of information and helps them to make sense of the patterns that surround them.

Coupled closely with building literacy around the consuming of story is the producing of story. Students who have an opportunity to produce narrative and story as a part of their learning reap both immediate and future benefits. Producing story can mean learning the best practices of oral storytelling. It can mean working through an iterative writing process to build the skills of writing story. It can also look like students synthesizing their learning through photos, videos, and infographics.

The producing of story brings to life the ideas and skills learned through the artful examination of the consuming of story. Schools looking to engage students in this area are providing explicit learning about both consuming and producing story, and in doing so, the learners in these schools, both students and adults, begin seeing through the lens of story as they move through daily life.

Modeling the power of storytelling is an essential skill for leaders and teacher leaders. It allows for connection, relationship, and empathy to grow in the learning ecosystem. Being open and transparent to the students and the community about moments of personal and professional perseverance builds trust. In addition, it models the power of story, provides students with the deeper connection that comes naturally from knowing someone's story, and begins to remove the fear of sharing story. This adult modeling also builds a community culture and spirit, where story is celebrated in the learning space.

For leaders, it is essential to lead out loud by talking through the decision-making process, placing ideas on the table, and explaining how actions and ideas fit together. Leaders need to be purposeful about the language that is used in all spaces and ask whether if there is a common story emerging from the building. Common language allows the story about the soul of a school to emerge. Leaders who are able to mold this story of their school will have deeper student engagement because the students will know the purpose of their learning.

Leaders will also have growing faculty engagement as they work toward a common mission supported by the compelling language. Finally, schools focusing on story will see an increase in community support as the community realizes that the success of the school comes from the narrative written by the school and not just the public scorecards for schools.

In building a school engaged and compelled by story, it is important to help the students build the skills of being catchers of story and crafters of story. Catchers of story are able to absorb the world of story that surrounds them. They see the world differently. They see the world as pictures and photos. They frame their observations with the eye of a photographer. Experiences are mental videos that are instantly edited, trimmed, and prepared for multiple audiences.

Students that know the power of story listen differently. They take a moment to breathe as they listen, so that their brain is absorbing story as opposed to thinking about the next thing to say. They have empathy for the storyteller as they try to place themselves in their shoes. This capacity to catch story grows for students as they see these behaviors modeled by their teachers and when they have time to practice. Catchers of story also need to have rich learning environments to practice these skills. This includes time on and off campus that surrounds the students with nature, beauty, and history.

Catchers of story begin to transition to crafters of story as they are given the space to reflect on their observations. Crafting stories usually begins as a journal entry or blog post for students. Crafting story allows students to make sense of life, have voice in a world that isn't ready to fully embrace their voice, and learn how to thread values and beliefs into the stories that are written. The varied media that students can use for storytelling and the crafting of story has grown tremendously in recent years. Students now have the opportunity to build powerful digital stories using creation and editing tools that until recently were reserved for professionals.

Building true capacity in this area means having the space and time needed for excellence. Students that are given the time to truly move through an iterative process will refine and revise with vigor. Students given choices on how to show their learning and showcase their voice and ideas will craft, craft, and craft story until excellence emerges. They will base their revisions on the feedback of peers, teachers, and the larger community and take time to compare their work to excellent exemplars that already exist.

Students learning to craft story also learn that the perfect story is never possible, but working through the crafting process with fidelity can bring students closer to a proficiency that will open doors. The doors that allow for others to hear their voice, see their talent in crafting message, and persuade others through the art of storytelling.

The power of story also brings additional gifts to learning spaces. Story, for schools, provides a counternarrative to the dominant narrative that schools are failing. Story is the reason that those polled in surveys give their personal schools a B, and schools in general a D or F because when the community knows and sees the story of their school, they know the successes, both big and small, and their grades rise to a B or better.

Story pushes back on the idea that schools are a place of danger and have no value in building the next generation of citizens, and students can also use story to build a counternarrative to push back the wave of narrative from the media that tends to marginalize the worth of kids and teens in society.

QUESTIONS FOR REFLECTION

Who is telling the story of your school?

How have you been explicit with modeling your storytelling with others?

Are you a catcher of story? Are you a crafter of story? How can you grow in this space?

RESOURCES

Books

Baldwin, Christina, *Storycatcher: Making Sense of Our Lives through the Power and Practice of Story* (New Word Library, 2007).

TED Talks

Adventures in Twitter Fiction, http://www.ted.com/talks/andrew_fitzgerald_adventures_in_twitter_fiction.html
The Danger of a Single Story, http://www.ted.com/talks/chimamanda_adichie_the_danger_of_a_single_story.html

Digital Storytelling

Center for Digital Storytelling, http://storycenter.org/
How to Use Digital Storytelling in Your Classroom, http://www.edutopia.org/digital-storytelling-classroom
Digital Storytelling in the Classroom, http://www.tech4learning.com/userfiles/file/pdfs/Frames/digital_storytelling/ds_classroom.pdf
The Educational Uses of Digital Storytelling, http://digitalliteracyintheclassroom.pbworks.com/f/Educ-Uses-DS.pdf
Digital Storytelling Resources, http://classroom-aid.com/technology-resources/digital-storytelling-resources/

FIFTEEN

The Science Project

Brad continued to look for ways to layer and nest the core work of his students and staff. This journey led him to the concept of citizen science, a growing set of opportunities, for kids and adults, to contribute to their community and science through data collection and observation. Throughout the world, top scientists studying a variety of topics are looking to the power and wisdom of the crowd to gather the data that they need to develop and test their hypotheses.

The expenses associated with travel and lodging are prohibitive for scientists gathering data in multiple locations, so, in many cases, they are calling on an army of citizens to support their work. This allows scientists to focus on data analysis as opposed to data collection as well as work on a greater number of projects simultaneously. Citizen science opportunities also provide students a chance to contribute to something larger than themselves.

Brad found his school's first citizen science project while he was wandering through the science museum. He was drawn to a display that showed students collecting algae from local ponds. The pictures showed kids dirty, wet, and smiling from ear to ear as they waded into the pond to collect muck. The project was sponsored by a local agribusiness that was looking to see if trace amounts of one of their products was showing up in the water supply of the community. They had always believed that their compound was self-destroying, but recent reports by an environmental watchdog organization showed different data.

Brad read through the notes on the display about how the company was trying to collect as much data as possible from various water sources, and the citizen science process was accelerating this. Brad took a picture of the two links on the display and returned to school with another idea on how to amplify the learning in the building.

He saw participation in this project as an opportunity to showcase the importance of the mathematical thinking that surrounds data collection, while reinforcing their mission of education for sustainability, and building an active, educated citizenry. Brad came to one of his student groups that met after school to discuss the idea of citizen science and the possibility of them piloting whether doing this type of project would support a greater interest in learning throughout the building. The club seemed interested.

A number of students went home and started exploring citizen science possibilities that night, and they found that there were hundreds of these projects happening simultaneously around the world. Some of the projects had just started while others had been going on for years. Two students met Brad at his car the next morning. They were talking so fast that he couldn't get a word in edgewise, but he eventually was able to say, "so citizen science might be a good thing." They continued without missing a beat by showing Brad one project that had to do with birds, another with flowers, and yet another with bees. They were ready to collect information, and they were ready to be "real scientists."

Brad had taught science for a long time, and he always struggled to get kids excited about the scientific method, exploring science in their own backyard, and talking and acting like real scientists. He had talked with his teachers about rewriting the science curriculum to focus on explorations and student-driven projects. Brad was convinced though that citizen science projects were not only ripe for engagement, but a golden opportunity for kids to connect to their community and be seen as assets. While meeting with two of the veteran science teachers in the building, Brad was surprised to find out that both of them had participated in citizen science projects last summer.

They talked about one of the most famous projects, the Cornell Bird Study, and how they were able to post data directly to the website, and even though their contribution was small, they recognized that having thousands of citizens working on this project created a big impact. They had pondered bridging the excitement of their experience and the learning in their classroom, but they weren't sure that taking two weeks to discuss birds was the right thing to do.

Together the teachers and Brad began to explore some of the projects that were available, and they were surprised by all of the opportunities for kids to learn through citizen science. They left the meeting looking at three projects that they thought fit into their curriculum with the least amount of redesign. The projects were a pollinator study on bees and their habitat, the pond study that Brad had seen in the science museum, and a study involving flowers and the time of year in which they bloomed.

Brad peeked into the classrooms that were working on the projects and realized that the students had collected data in ten to twenty different ways, and the students were trying to figure out the difference between having data and having data that can be educative for the study and larger audiences. The conversation around data collection was rich, and the students realized that the world has lots of data, but too often it is inaccessible to others because the narrative that explains the data isn't weaved through the numbers in a way that brings the message to life.

The students decided that they would build their data sets in collaborative spaces so that they had anytime access and the ability to share across teams. This breakthrough seemed to bring coherence to the project. The volume of useable data increased tremendously as the teams made the connections necessary on the best ways to collect and organize the data.

The classes were now ready for their internal reviews. The groups would each give a short Ignite presentation on their findings. Ignite presentations are six minutes long and slides are auto-forwarded every 20 seconds. This method keeps the audience's attention high, while forcing the speakers to prioritize their talking points. It gets a lot of ideas into the learning space in a short amount of time.

The teachers then decided to ask students to conduct a second round of feedback gathering. For this, students participated in critical friends groups that provided feedback on how to best collect, report, and share their data. It was important in these spaces that students move from being nice and nonconfrontational to providing the formative feedback necessary to better shape the future of the project.

The second phase of the data review would be for students to contact an expert in the field and ask for an opportunity to talk through their process and purpose. The students were very tentative about reaching out to adults and especially adults with expertise in their learning topic. Brad was able to dig into his network of colleagues that existed outside of education to connect his students to open and willing professionals who understood the mission of the project.

For students, this review brought deeper feedback and most important an authentic audience that again raised the quality of the work. The students were finally able to enter their data into the citizen science database, and they left the project feeling as though they had made a contribution to their community and beyond. They also built a greater understanding around what it meant to be a scientist. They had moved their mental models away from white lab coats and beakers.

They now realized that at the core of being a scientist was the need to be connected to the community as it is the only way that scientists could truly make sense of the world. Brad would extend the citizen science opportunities for students as the years continued, and he hoped to be able to make citizen science an avenue for drawing families and community members into the learning process. For now, though, he was excited to see student engagement swelling around these opportunities.

QUESTIONS FOR REFLECTION

Are students seen as an asset or a liability in your community?

What science learning opportunities are available in your community?

Where do students get internal and external feedback about their work in your current system?

SIXTEEN
Empowering Citizen Scientists

The mental model of student as liability is a mindset for many adults. This mental model is reinforced when students are loitering near restaurants, stealing from the grocery store, vandalizing the park, or being a nuisance at a local event. The narrative that is perpetuated paints students as rebellious, having a lack of appreciation for the things that are provided, and lacking a respect for rules and procedures. Though this may apply to some small slice of students, the majority of students are community assets in a variety of ways.

As a school leader, it is essential to build a counternarrative to these mental models, and one way to begin this process is to develop ways for students to be connected to their community. Students that are involved in projects that bring solutions to a community are able to shift the way that adults outside of school perceive them. In addition, they begin to see the power of their voice, and the opportunity that they have to affect change.

One strategy that begins to craft the idea that students are a community asset is the use of citizen science. Citizen science relies on the collection of data by citizens to support research in a variety of areas of science. Schools that are using citizen science are seeing student engagement grow, specifically around many of the environmental science issues in their community. In addition, this opportunity provides a space for learning about data collection, data analysis, the scientific method, persuasion strategies, public speaking, presentation skills, and infographic development.

According to the European Commission report on Environmental Citizen Science, the term *citizen science* was first used by social scientist Alan Irwin, in his 1995 book *Citizen Science*, to describe expertise that exists among those who are traditionally seen as ignorant "lay people." More

71

recently, the term *citizen cyberscientist* has emerged as more and more citizen science is taking place by the reporting of data using smartphones, laptops, and tablets. Though it was 1995 when the term *citizen science* was birthed, science by amateurs has been taking place for centuries. For example, Charles Darwin, the famous explorer and father of the theory of evolution, had no scientific training, yet he contributed deeply to the canon of scientific knowledge.

The Citizen Science Alliance has worked to bring learners, both in schools and outside of schools, together to scale the work of citizen science. It is estimated that nearly three hundred projects are taking place around the world to support a variety of science research projects. The Citizen Science Alliance's mission is to create online citizen science projects that involve the public in academic research.

The increasing demand for data in science has outstripped the capacity of researchers. Though technology can play an essential role in closing this data gap, there is a growing need for citizen scientists, and students can play a significant role in meaningful science by participating in these projects. Another advantage for researchers working on these projects is that by having humans doing the observations, they can observe beyond the scope of the intended observation. This gives scientists the opportunity to have a richer understanding of the patterns that surround the data as well.

The Citizen Science Alliance sees a number of key advantages to citizen science projects. These include the ability to deal with very large data sets, the ability to gather data from multiple points of view (which can limit bias and error in the collection process through the wisdom of crowds), the opportunity to fine-tune the technology needed to analyze large amounts of data, and the "serendipitous discovery" that comes from humans keeping an eye out for the weird and odd in the most routine of data collection situations.

As schools evolve in their journey with citizen science, some are choosing to launch their own projects and become the hub for the data collection. This approach allows students to begin to manage a loose network of citizen scientists from throughout their community and beyond. Taking leadership on a project where both students and adults are contributing to gathering data around a topic helps students grow their sense of power and vision for how they can make positive contributions to their community and be seen as an asset.

Researcher Rick Bonney outlines a nine-step process for developing a citizen science project. This process includes choosing a scientific question; forming a scientist/educator/technologist/evaluator team; developing, testing, and refining protocols, data forms, and educational support materials; recruiting participants; training participants; accepting, editing, and displaying data; analyzing and interpreting data; disseminating results; and measuring outcomes.

Two of the longest-running projects in the citizen science realm are the Audubon Society's Christmas Bird Count that began in North America in 1900 with twenty-seven participants. It is still running today and attracts thousands of participants, including many schools across the country. The second is the SETI@Home (Search for Extraterrestrial Intelligence) project that launched in 1999 with the purpose of using excess computer capacity to search the stars on more frequencies and with more sensitivity. This project basically uses the computers of thousands of citizen scientists to create a virtual supercomputer for its deep search of the universe.

The GLOBE Program is another example of citizen science that allows schools the opportunity to work on a variety of projects. Topics include atmosphere, earth as a system, hydrology, land cover/biology, and soil. This program boasts a community of 250,000 citizen scientists as well as "the infrastructure to support massively distributed citizen science, which can cope with the rigours of hosting the most popular projects." The GLOBE Program has become a great launching point for school leaders looking to grow their citizen science capacity without having to redevelop all of the structures and procedures needed to create new citizen science projects.

The GLOBE Program also provides professional development and training for educators interested in citizen science through cost-free regional workshops and online training. GLOBE has developed a teacher's guide that is used to train teachers in the protocols and learning activities that comprise the scaffolded K–12 GLOBE curriculum.

They have materials that include a wide variety of classroom and field activities to help students place their measurements in a broader context and relate their own local observations to global environmental issues. The GLOBE Program also brings students together from around the world to discuss their observation, data analysis, and passion surrounding the projects.

Citizen science has grown tremendously over the past decade, but there is still space for school leaders and lead learners to wrap this learning into their daily lessons. Wiggins and Crowston encourage teachers to choose the right type of project for them and their students. They break the types of projects into five groups: action, conservation, investigation, virtual, and educational.

Action projects have students collaborating with scientists on action research on mostly local environmental issues. Conservation projects focus on managing natural resources. Investigation projects focus on answering scientific questions, and virtual projects have similar aims to the types above, but they are carried out remotely or using online learning. Finally, educational projects are those that have less of a focus on the science and more on informing or educating the citizen scientists.

Many schools participating in these projects are being thoughtful in balancing the green time and screen time that must take place when it comes to citizen science. The use of technology can heighten engagement with the concepts and ideas surrounding the citizen science project, but it can also be a barrier to experiencing the natural world, observing without filter, and being present in the data collection process. School leaders who are working to bring deeper levels of engagement should discuss with staff about how to best balance the work of their citizen cyberscientists.

No matter where a school begins on this journey, the results will feature students highly engaged and energized. Students who are participating are busy looking for solutions, supporting the struggles of their community, and realizing that their contribution to science could make a difference. Eventually, the story of this work is told to the community and a natural shift begins as those outside the school see the potential of students. They hear student voice, and feel the passion of students to make the community better. Slowly the mental model shifts, and the students, empowered and in full voice, are recognized as assets to their community.

QUESTIONS FOR REFLECTION

What efforts are you taking to move your students from appearing as liabilities to being assets in your community?

How is science real for your students? How are they contributing to something greater?

How are you allowing your students to feel empowered?

In what ways can students make an impact in your community? How do they have voice?

RESOURCES

Scientific American, http://www.scientificamerican.com/citizen-science/

SETI@home, http://setiathome.berkeley.edu/sah_about.php

Report to European Commission on Environmental Citizen Science, http://ec.europa.eu/environment/integration/research/newsalert/pdf/IR9.pdf

Cornell Lab of Ornithology, http://www.birds.cornell.edu/citsci/

Citizen Science Alliance, http://www.citizensciencealliance.org/philosophy.html

The Globe Program, http://www.globe.gov/about-globe/how-globe-works

From Conservation to Crowdsourcing: A Typology of Citizen Science, http://crowston.syr.edu/system/files/hicss-44.pdf

Understanding Citizen Science and Environmental Monitoring, http://www.ceh.ac.uk/products/publications/documents/citizensciencereview.pdf

Public Participation in Scientific Research: Defining the Field and Assessing Its Potential for Informal Science Education, http://www.birds.cornell.edu/citscitoolkit/publications/CAISE-PPSR-report-2009.pdf

SEVENTEEN

Unlocking the Past, Engaging the Future

The first time that Brad heard about the international design competition in his hometown he was very intrigued. It wasn't often that design teams from around the world were looking for a solution to poverty and neighborhood decay in his backyard. The space being examined for the competition had a storied history in the community, one that was larger than even Brad knew in the beginning. Following the Depression, many urban areas including Brad's city were filled with wide swaths of poverty that contained substandard housing, poor sanitation, and inadequate utilities.

Over the next few years, as part of President Roosevelt's New Deal, cities had new federal resources to begin crafting solutions, and one of the most heralded solutions of the time was the development of modular high-rise housing that would eliminate the issues of quality of housing, sanitation, and utilities, while also "reclaiming" large tracts of land for redevelopment. One perspective of this effort shined a bright light on the project's intentions to help the poor and needy, while another version portrayed the effort as a land grab by wealthy urban planners to build on valuable land.

No matter the version of history that was true, the reality was that the construction of these "homes" would fail the community over time. In the case of Brad's city, the housing built in the 1950s would implode in the 1970s, and since then, the site has sat fallow. It was reclaimed by nature, and had become an unplanned urban forest. It was in this space that the design competition would play out over the next nine months.

Two of Brad's teachers also saw the design competition information, and they approached Brad about the possibility of building learning around this opportunity. There were initially more questions than answers as Brad and his teachers explored how to begin this process, but even in these uncomfortable moments, all of them had a gut feeling that something great could emerge from this experience. Brad was starting to see many more of his teachers bringing these ideas to the table. They were looking for ways to engage kids, energize learning, and most important, make the world their classroom.

Brad felt that this interest in bringing new ideas to the table came from a growing sense of trust between the leadership and staff around the many philosophical changes that had taken place at the school over the past few years. No matter the cause, Brad knew his organization was making a shift. The ideas and concepts he and his teachers had talked about and struggled with were now the very same ideas that were defining the culture of the school.

Looking to truly make this learning interdisciplinary, Brad approached one of his elective teachers about being the project manager. He told her that she would have all the resources and time that she needed to make this project a huge success. Brad also worked with her to find the connections to the standards and curriculum that would help to thread this project into the other learning moments across subjects throughout the year. They also decided that the primary goal of the project was to showcase that learning beyond the classroom walls can be both a powerful and rigorous experience.

To get more information about how to participate, the teacher reached out to the coordinator of the design competition. She asked if it would be possible for the students to first hear about the project from him as she knew that having someone outside the school launch the project would add to the excitement around the learning. The coordinator offered a better idea. He offered to take the students on a site visit to the location of the design competition, discuss the history of the site, allow them to take pictures, and answer their questions.

In addition, he mentioned to the teacher that the students may get value in seeing the excellent documentary surrounding the rise and fall of this site as it provided insights on the people that lived through this experience. The teacher saw both of these opportunities as a way to bring energy to the project. The visuals of both the documentary and being on location would aid the students in seeing the potential impact of their work.

As these kickoff events approached, the teacher shared some initial guiding questions that she envisioned students would build upon as the days progressed. She offered these questions: Which parts of history should we forget and which should we remember? How do we preserve history with new design and building? What are the core elements of a community? The teacher gave the students space to struggle with these ideas, and she knew that their understanding would multiply as their experiences in this project grew.

Prior to their site visit, the students went to the school's theater to watch the documentary. This documentary looked at the rise and fall of this grand project on the site of the current design competition. It showcased personalities, emotions, and faces of the families who lived through this experience. The viewing allowed the students to empathize with the characters of the movie. They were able to see that working on this design competition was an opportunity to shape the future of a place that had a complicated past. Following the viewing, the teachers were able to get the director and producer of the movie, who happened to be local, to visit the classroom to discuss their work.

The students learned that the stories in the movie were but a fraction of the stories that were collected. The director talked about the difficulty of his role. He had to make sense of all of the information, while shaping and trimming what would make the final movie, without losing the multiple perspectives of the story. He saw himself as the curator of story, and he explained to the students the importance of recognizing that all things are biased, but part of his role with this film was to minimize that.

After watching the movie, the students were very excited to visit the site, but little did they know how this experience would shape their learning. The bus dropped the students off on a street corner that had no signs of life. The students walked a short distance and crossed over a chain-link fence that ringed the property. Immediately, their senses were engaged. The guide was wise not to begin talking for almost four minutes as the students wandered toward the center of the property.

The students were observing, taking pictures, and commenting quietly as not to ruin the aural chemistry of the moment. It was clear that they were trying to breathe in the moment and pull history from the remains. The guide for the visit started by talking about why the design competition was taking place. The group sponsoring the competition saw incredible potential for the neighborhood and its churches and schools that surrounded the parameter. Even though it was currently in a less than desirable state (it was now home to stray dogs, squatters, and native plants), they felt renewal to this space could go a long way to anchoring sustainable change in this section of town.

The students returned to school to begin their work on the project. Together the students and teacher decided that the final display of learning would be both the design competition submission as well as a presentation of learning for students and parents. In small teams, students were looking at a variety of aspects of how the past, present, and future of this site spoke to the essential questions of the project. The teacher surrounded the students with experts from throughout the area including university professors, urban planners, activists, and more. Each of these experts worked closely with the teacher and students to enrich the learning environment.

One of the experts brought into the project was an area architectural firm that supported the students. They became teammates weaving the ideas of the students into beautiful final displays and supporting the submission entry all the way to the end. Brad and the teachers involved were so thankful for the support of the architecture firm and the community.

The students submitted to the contest, but didn't make the final ten. Many of the students struggled throughout the project, but they all acknowledged that complex, messy, authentic work creates deep learning. Brad and the teachers had now built a model of structures, routines, and procedures that other teachers and students could replicate in the future. Most important, Brad, his teachers, and the students believed that learning with the community held great promise for the mission of the school.

QUESTIONS FOR REFLECTION

Where have you lead a synergy between subjects that has energized kids?

Are you the leader in the building that people approach when they are looking for new resources or fresh ideas?

How are you growing your students' connection to the community past, present, and future?

EIGHTEEN
Learning beyond the Classroom

The current mental construct of a classroom is an element of fiction and history. It is a relic and ready for its place in school museums around the world. This classroom that features a teacher's desk, student desks in rows, and writing on a chalkboard or whiteboard is unfortunately still the norm in today's schoolhouses. As learning has evolved, the places of learning have not.

There are few places in the world where if someone woke up from a fifty-year nap they would feel comfortable, but the classrooms of many of our schools would be one of these places. Children deserve to learn in beautiful spaces that support learning, and teachers deserve the opportunity to use their surroundings to enhance their lessons and motivate greater inquiry and passion in the hearts of their students.

The idea of thinning the walls of the classroom isn't a new concept in education. In reality, most ideas in education aren't new, but instead they are evolving to new heights, reaching new schools, and hopefully growing in comfort for more and more educators around the country. Thinning the walls of the classroom or building permeable schools has grown in its complexity over the past twenty years as educators and learners are now able to have almost unlimited access to information beyond their classroom and textbooks.

No longer is a teacher destined to be the dispenser of the best information as the world is now providing the best resources. This should allow classrooms to be places to make sense of information, curate information, and mold information into new forms of learning to be shared with others. Students that aren't experiencing this type of learning are in a decelerated learning space at a time when the potential for acceleration is immense.

Learning beyond the classroom brings energy to learning that is engaging for students. It brings context to learning and continues to address why the learning matters. Learning beyond the classroom brings students to the experts and experts to the students. Learning beyond the classroom is a mindset for the instructional toolbox that opens the doors to learning in the hallways, on the playgrounds, in the community, and with classrooms around the globe.

This mindset can also transfer into a lifelong learning skill for students where they feel liberated to seek their own answers, ask their own questions, and pursue learning in which they are passionate. Education thought leader Will Richardson believes that learning beyond the classroom has three starting points: "thinning the classroom walls, being transparent, and talking to strangers."

The easiest way to thin the classroom walls is to get out of the classroom. This means breaking the routine and the inertia of the classroom being the primary learning space. Principals and other school leaders can model this by taking staff meetings outside; taking staff into the community for observation, events, and service learning; and making home visits to connect with families. After these experiences, leaders should take time to reflect with staff about the feelings, emotions, and growth that came from this break in the routine. The leader also has an opportunity in this space to ask questions about how teachers could bring these types of experiences to students. Thin classroom walls also bring the strengths and challenges of a community into the learning space. It means bringing the problems and issues of the community into the classroom while keeping it a sanctuary for students that need time to escape the stresses of life. Schools with this philosophy recognize, through conversations and activities, that life is school and school is life, and that the issues of both are tangled. School leaders and others looking to thin the walls of their school should remember that doing so comes with a need to thin the walls of their hearts.

Teacher Jenna Shaw said this best. "I will strive to thin the walls of not only my classroom, but my heart. When my heart is open is when the real learning happens. Let's open our hearts together and discover a deeper truth about ourselves and our world."

Thinning the classroom walls also means allowing others to learn with the students in the schools. Technology integration now allows more and more learning between schools and co-learning between clusters of schools. This helps to bring students into engaging learning spaces that they wouldn't have been able to experience in their school or community. Classrooms are attending concerts, experiments, meetings, and virtual field trips beyond their classroom as teachers see themselves as resource providers and facilitators. More and more of those resources are now coming from the greater marketplace of ideas.

Communities want to support their schools. There is an almost universal desire by communities to see their schools succeed. As school leaders, it is important to press more and more of the story of the school, its mission, and its daily life into a public space as resources from the community are attracted to this level of transparency. As schools showcase that they have a learning narrative that includes the community and that it longs to bring partners into the equation, the village will wrap around the school. Transparency also allows the community to see the complexity of public education. School leaders and excellent schools can make educating students look easy.

The reality is that leading and learning in an effective school is complex, and the community needs to have the veil of simplicity removed for a greater understanding of modern schooling to be realized. Being transparent with student work and student voice brings a beauty to the education happening inside the school walls, and it also allows a bright light to shine on the excellent teaching at the school. Teachers can also benefit from greater transparency as it provides a larger audience for them to find their voice, advocate for their passions, and support students in the school and community. Transparency doesn't come with a lifetime supply of blemish cream though.

School leaders looking to connect their classroom with their community will be showing the messy parts of education as well. Transparency can mean losing some control of the message, learning to apologize to a larger audience for mistakes, and embracing the hard and strange conversations that can come from those who don't embrace the vision. Even with these challenges, transparency engages all learners as they feel the energy and support of the community wrapping around them.

Will Richardson uses the phrase "talking with strangers" to push school leaders and learners to embrace the fact that the best resources for kids lie beyond the classroom. For years, the mantra "don't talk to strangers" has filled our schools with the intended purpose of keeping our kids safe, and it still remains a good idea, but the difference is that talking to strangers and learning from strangers are two different ways of thinking. As the crowdsourcing of knowledge becomes the most powerful way to gather real-time information about topics, emergencies, and current events, school leaders have to prepare students to learn in this way.

This can be modeled through adult learning in social media spaces. School leaders and lead learners should be learning from educators around the country who do their job better than they do. This means finding allies and colleagues who can support and grow their leadership, serve as a sounding board for ideas, and support positive risk taking.

This professional learning network should also transfer into the students' learning spaces. Students should be learning from other students with similar passions throughout the country as they work collaboratively on highly engaging, student-centered projects. This is the value that comes from the strangers that exist outside of the classroom. Learning from strangers also brings new perspectives and new energy to those dusty and worn ideas in the learning repertoire of even the best teachers.

Students who are learning from others outside of the classroom also feel empowered as they realize that they have access to the best information, experts, and ideas on the topics of their choosing. The road to life-long learning comes from this type of empowerment for students.

The next generation of learning that includes learning beyond the classroom, permeable schools, and the thinning of classroom walls remains in its infancy in a lot of ways. It is a concept though that has the force of innovative education behind it. It also fits deeply with the philosophy of David Price, the author of *Open*, who talks about the growing open nature of all systems including schools. Price, in *Open*, pushes schools to lean into this open way of thinking. He sees it as a force that has been released and isn't going back into its box. Open classrooms, open schools, and open communities have a chance to truly reshape learning spaces as we know them.

QUESTIONS FOR REFLECTION

What strangers have you talked to in your learning journey recently?

What steps could your students take to be more public and transparent with their learning?

What unfiltered parts of your teaching have you made public?

How could you use a "learning beyond the classroom" model to attract more resources to your school?

RESOURCES

Will Richardson on learning beyond the classroom, http://learning.blogs.nytimes.com/2012/10/25/guest-post-three-starting-points-for-thinking-differently-about-learning/?_r=0
Jenna Shaw on learning beyond the classroom, http://edtechadventure.blogspot.com/2013/11/thinning-walls-of-our-hearts.html
Price, David, *Open: How We'll Work, Live and Learn in the Future*, Kindle edition (Crux Publishing, 2013).

NINETEEN

A Place to Make

The work that the teachers and students were doing at Brad's school was building positive energy. Schools and teachers from throughout the community were asking questions about how this school was able to break the mold and find new, bold ways to get kids excited about their learning. It was becoming more and more common for visitors to be working with Brad's teachers, sitting in classes, and collaborating at high levels. This momentum buoyed the initiatives that were taking root and provided some external motivation to strive for excellence.

Brad knew that this was the perfect time to press forward with some additional initiatives that could make his school the place in which he had dreamed. He knew that the next steps would lock the greater vision together and push the teachers into new spaces. He also knew that the next steps would be the most uncomfortable for some as the common belief that all students can and will learn at high levels would be tested.

Brad began to show his staff some important data about a blind spot that was emerging. The school had about fifteen students who were not finding success in their current learning journey, and they had an additional thirty students who were marginally successful. Brad's definition of success was broader than a normal set of academic metrics based on students' summative assessments. He was also looking at student work rate and student portfolios. Each of these measures showed students who had moments of engagement, energy, and production at school, but they weren't getting the learning experience that Brad felt would be necessary for them to be successful in high school and beyond.

Staying dedicated to this group of students is the most difficult part of being a school leader, but he also realized that this was central to his shift from being a place-holding manager to being a courageous leader. He met with a small group of teachers to talk about his vision in this area. It was an "open thought" meeting. Teachers now understood that this was the type of meeting where all ideas were on the table and that Brad was truly searching for a better road forward based on the wisdom of the room.

He asked a lot of questions, tinkered with a number of ideas, drew on the white board, and listened for nuggets of possibility to emerge. This type of meeting was fantastic for teachers who liked to wander through the possibilities, but it was frustrating for others who were looking for immediate direction, a to-do list, or concrete steps to a solution. Brad realized this, and tried to balance supporting those uncomfortable in this space while helping this same group grow into this way of learning. He was always looking for a better balance to these meetings to help everyone.

During these initial meetings on supporting this group of students, ideas did emerge and eventually consensus grew. The first area of consensus was that this group of students needed additional time to move while learning. One teacher told the story about a student who frequently came to school with a very flat affect, but every time she saw him in physical education, participating in outside learning, or helping others his internal energy tank was brimming over.

Another teacher mentioned that many of the students that they were trying to reach were doodlers and illustrators, and he was sure that they had a lot of creativity even though he was struggling to harness it for learning in his classroom. Brad and the teachers also knew that many of these students were playing games that asked them to create and design using their spatial intelligence. The final thread that was emerging was that many of these students had an incredible focus in those moments when they were actually engaged in their learning. It was rare that the teacher saw this in the students, but in these moments, they were completely entranced in their learning.

All of these factors led Brad to consider bringing a fresh learning space to his school that could potentially deeply engage these kids and the others. Like most good ideas that start as interventions, they end up being good for all kids. Brad and his teachers would use the next three months to build the ideal makerspace for their kids. The concept of the makerspace wasn't a new approach when Brad started it. Schools and communities around the country were embracing the idea of teaching entrepreneurship, design thinking, and manufacturing through the makerspace concept.

The project started with taking an old classroom that had become a storage closet filled with books, technology, and supplies from another era, and opening up the space for design. Once empty, Brad brought groups of students, teachers, and community members together in the space and posed a single question, "What resources would this space need to be a center for ideas and innovation in our learning community?"

As it always seems to occur in these conversations in which students are invited, the kids were incredibly insightful. They talked about comfortable seats, whiteboards for planning, having real tools to use, and being careful to recycle and reuse as many materials as possible. The students wanted the space to be "gracefully messy."

The teachers talked about opportunities to build, revise, iterate, and store projects over time. They also talked about bringing in some of the newest technology tools to the space like 3D printers and milling machines. They talked about how this could be a space for adult learning as well. The community members were intrigued that a school would allow students to learn in this way. Members of the community shared stories of their favorite moments in school, and most of them had to do with big projects, creating, and designing.

They talked about the screwdriver that they made in shop class and the sets that they painted and designed for the school play. Brad took copious notes throughout these sessions. He wanted it to be an inspirational space that had a magnetic effect on students. He wanted this space to be known as the place where ideas come to grow.

Three months later, the space was in play. The soft opening of the space had students creating something for Mother's Day. Some of them drew and painted, while other students used the tools available to create. Some students dove right in, and others carefully took time to draw their design and think through how they would proceed. In all cases, kids were highly engaged in learning.

There were a lot of "mistakes" on the floor, literally; paper and supplies littered the floor as the students followed the motto on the wall that read Fail Faster, Fail Forward. Brad couldn't be happier to see his students loving this new space. The real trick would be to move it from novelty to deep learning that engaged all kids, especially the ones who didn't take to some of the traditional learning methods at the school.

The grand opening for the space was right before the end of the school year. Brad and his staff were intentional about making this a community-wide event by including alumni, senior citizens, business leaders, and parents. The evening was a chance not only to showcase the new space, but to have people discuss how the space could grow, and think about what resources could best support the work.

Brad made it clear that it was designed for the community, and it would always be a space in flux so as to generate positive change. The community loved the space, and it was the talk of the local newspaper for a couple of weeks. Brad knew that having this space was an opportunity to continue to tell the story that his school had a broader definition of success than other schools.

As the new school year dawned, the makerspace was ready for the first day. All of the teachers were trained on how to use the tools. Each of the teachers also took some time to think about three levels of projects.

The first was an opportunity for all students to create in the makerspace. Brad was dedicated to having all students participate in this form of learning during the first quarter.

In addition, Brad asked his teachers to build a project that would allow students the option of using the makerspace to showcase their learning. His hope was that the students with less than ideal engagement the previous year would gravitate into using this space for their learning. The final project that Brad wanted his teachers to envision was a long-term project that involved iteration over the course of the students' careers at the school.

The makerspace had plenty of bins and drawers to house work over time, and Brad knew that excellence was found in work over time. The first year ended with many of these goals achieved. Students were learning by doing and exploring. Students were collaborating on projects and beginning to think of ways to use the makerspace for projects outside of school as well. Brad had the start of another avenue for engagement for all students to experience deep learning.

QUESTIONS FOR REFLECTION

What would you like to try to do to support struggling learners in your learning space?

What spaces do you have that could be transformed into engaging spaces for learning?

What do you see as Brad's next spaces to build a culture of making at his school?

TWENTY

Making Things Better

Though some would venture that the skill of making things better is an inherent part of people's DNA, the reality is that growing students into the makers of the future begins with the decisions of school leaders. Head to a preschool, park, or playground in the community and take some time to watch kids at play. They are making forts, castles, structures from blocks, and imaginary worlds in the open space of play that they are provided.

The level of engagement in these spaces is complete, total, and beautiful to see. Kids are deeply immersed in creating the spaces that they want to explore as well as looking for ways to make things better. Formal learning spaces need to mirror these experiences to prepare students for an emerging economy where the money to be made is, according to Cory Doctorow in his book *Makers*, like krill. He states that the new way for individuals to support themselves will include a billion little entrepreneurial opportunities, like the krill in the ocean, that can be discovered and cobbled together to support a lifestyle.

Chris Anderson, a former editor for *Wired* magazine and author of *Makers: The New Industrial Revolution*, outlines how a growing movement of individuals are looking at manufacturing in a completely different way. This group of makers are finding a niche for production that is smaller than the average factory that produces thousands of pieces for sale but larger than the single, handcrafted, personalized item.

This "small batch" production or right-sized manufacturing is being made possible by advances in open source sharing of techniques, plans, and ideas coupled with production tools like 3D printers, technology-rich design and engineering tools, and crowd sourced financing options like Kickstarter and Fundly that allow entrepreneurs to cobble together small donations from around the world to support new, innovative ideas.

This revolution in manufacturing and design demands new skills in today's learners. Many school leaders have identified this shift and started the process of bringing making into a greater part of the mission of the school. For many schools, this begins with carving out a makerspace. Part shop, part design studio, and part idea incubator, the school makerspace is a new type of classroom for the new creativity needed.

Makerspace.com sees makerspaces as community centers with tools that combine manufacturing equipment and passion-based learning for the purpose of enabling community members to design, prototype, and create manufactured works that wouldn't be possible to make with the resources available to individuals working alone. For them, making represents the democratization of design, engineering, fabrication, and education. An essential part of the maker movement is the design thinking process.

Over the past decade, the Institute of Design at Stanford University, or the d.school, has showcased how design thinking feeds into the maker movement and ultimately how design thinking has the potential to support large-scale social change. School leaders who are considering bringing additional making into their learning spaces to maximize engagement should think about not only the space needed to bring reality to this strategy, but the mindset and processes needed to bring creative confidence into the learning space.

The d.school has built a group of mindsets into their practices that are essential elements for any school wrapping design and making into their work. They are show, don't tell; focus on human values; embrace experimentation; craft clarity; be mindful of process; have bias toward action; and collaborate radically. Not many schools today can say that they are deeply embracing these, but there are schools that are looking at these mindsets as a way to break the current inertia of schooling and begin to drive engagement into the heart of the learning.

These mindsets, coupled with the design thinking process, allow students and educators to get the most from the space set aside for making in their building. The design thinking process includes five phases or modes that work together to surface problems and solutions for making a school, community, or planet a better place for learning, living, and growing. It starts with empathy. According to the d.school process, empathy is the foundation of a human-centered design process.

Empathy occurs by observing users and their behavior in context, engaging users through conversation, and immersing those in the design process in the user's experience. Schools that have successfully placed makerspaces in their learning ecosystem have an initial boost of engagement based on the new "toys," but schools with sustainable growth in their makerspace, where exploration and deep learning are occurring, have a school culture comfortable with empathy being at the core of the design thinking process.

The second mode of the design thinking process is to define. Beyond the normal understanding of the concept of define, this mode pushes those involved in the process to focus and synthesize the information gathered during the empathy findings into an actionable problem statement known as the point of view or POV. This phase, when completed with the level of detail necessary to bring clarity to the process, helps to avoid a loss of focus that can naturally occur as the manufacturing of solutions begins to take place.

Schools and leaders looking to see these phases in action can turn to a design organization like IDEO, led by David and Tom Kelley. The Kelley brothers have published *Creative Confidence: Unleashing the Creative Potential Within Us All*, a book that showcases the duty of schools to focus on making, design thinking, and building creative confidence to meet the learning needs of the students in the future.

The final three modes of design thinking are ideate, prototype, and test. These are the heart of the work in the makerspace. Ideate feeds off the focus of the point of view, but instead of going deeper, it switches gears to go wider. Beyond the traditional brainstorming for solutions, the ideate mode is designed to bring diversity to the potential solutions and drive the solution sets to new heights beyond the obvious. It is a time to "uncover unexpected areas of exploration."

Ideation is the beginning of the messy process of making. Folks entering a makerspace during the ideation mode may see multiple white boards with ideas and mind maps and hundreds of sticky notes on walls and surfaces, and there may be drawings on large rolls of paper with arrows connecting dots between ideas and possibilities.

At this point, it is time for rapid prototyping to occur. This begins to bring ideas to life. Ideas begin to take a physical form. This can be models created from the tools in the makerspace like the 3D printer, or it can be detailed storyboards or a role-play that brings the idea to life. Prototyping takes the ideate mode and moves the conversation from theoretical to practical. In this mode, there is new learning, the start of fresh conversations, and the opportunity to fail forward before moving into the implementation of a solution.

Failing forward and learning how to fail are key elements to the prototyping stage of design thinking. This is where some of the greatest learning for adults and students can take place as it often means scrapping one idea and returning to other ideas for fresh inspiration. Wrapped into this phase is testing. This brings the design process and the making process full circle as the potential solution is brought back to the user for consideration. Often learners realize that the solution must be fine-tuned, combined, or reengineered.

Many of today's young learners will be self-employed, by working for themselves on a variety of projects simultaneously. They will need to be nimble with their support for others and bring creative solutions to the table. Learning in a makerspace begins this way of thinking and way of life. Makerspaces also connect the mind and body. Students who are doing, building, and making are feeling a connection to their learning that brings belly fire and energy to education.

It allows learning in schools to reach the levels of engagement that are seen in the imaginative play in the sandbox or at the park. Schools and classrooms that are "making" today are making sure that the garden of solutions needed for communities and the planet are being tended to for the next generation and beyond.

QUESTIONS FOR REFLECTION

How can making be a value-added piece of the instructional processes in your classroom, school, and community?

What pieces of the design thinking process are already embedded in your work and which need to grow as a part of your work?

What physical space could be used to build a makerspace?

What role does learning how to fail play in the success of your students?

RESOURCES

Makerspace, http://makerspace.com/
Make magazine, http://makezine.com/
Doctorow, Cory, *Makers* (Tor Books, 2009).
Anderson, Chris, *Makers: The New Industrial Revolution* (Crown Business, 2014).
Maker Shed: the official store of *Make* magazine, http://www.makershed.com/?gclid=CID85a6z7bsCFUgS7Aod9DAAXg
Disruption Department, http://thedisruptiondepartment.org/
Stanford Design School, K12 Lab, http://www.k12lab.org/
IDEO, www.ideo.com/
Kelley, Tom, and David Kelley, *Creative Confidence: Unleashing the Creative Potential Within Us All* (Crown Business, 2011).
Agency by Design, http://www.pz.gse.harvard.edu/agency_by_design.php

TWENTY-ONE

Finding the Edge through Empathy

Brad had seen an incredible shift in the passion and energy of the staff and students. He realized that his desire and passion to have a school that maximized engagement and fostered innovation was also a desire of those in the surrounding community. The new energy was being embraced and cultivated throughout the learning spaces. Brad celebrated the changes, and he began to examine ways to continue the momentum and leverage excellence from this new system.

He examined all of the systems in the school looking for gaps, holes, and opportunities. In this time of reflection and deep introspection about the school, he had a conversation with a library assistant. She was sharing how important the concept of community had grown in her life recently. She talked about how deeply she felt connected at home with family, at church, and in this school community. She said that she could feel the soul in each of these spaces. She then asked Brad what he thought made this school so soulful and whether he felt the same deep connection. Brad gave a quick response that he, too, felt the same connection without really thinking about the question.

Later that night, Brad returned to this conversation. Brad knew that learning was at the center of his work, and that schools, in their best moments, foster creativity, critical thinking, and collaboration. Brad also knew that the learning environment was only as good as its relational foundation meaning, how the kids related to the kids, how the adults related to the kids, and how the ecosystem supported all of the nutrients in the system.

At the core of these relationships, Brad found empathy. Brad knew that the greater the empathy capacity of the school, the deeper the successes would be now and in the future. The soul of this school was empathy, and Brad knew he had to find deeper ways to tend to the soul. After spending so many days of his career working on situations where kids had treated other kids poorly, Brad was aware of the deep need for helping students navigate these waters.

For a long time, he had found himself trapped in a reactionary space moving from incident to incident and phone call to phone call without a true vision of how to step in front of the train and fix the tracks. Brad thought that building a culture of empathy could be a step in the right direction, but as promising as it sounded, he had no idea where to start, so instead of talking, he set up opportunities to listen.

As a leader, Brad knew that it was hard to facilitate and listen at the same time, so he called a friend at a neighboring school to facilitate these sessions for him. The design would be a fishbowl format with three layers of conversations. The first group would have the adults in the middle discussing their perspective on bullying in the school. The second group would have the students discussing how people being treated poorly impacts their school. The final group would be a self-selecting group of adults and students who felt like they wanted to come to the center to discuss solutions to the issues that they had heard.

Over the course of a month, four of these sessions would be completed, and Brad was able to videotape the sessions, which allowed him to be present in the conversations as opposed to participating in his default principal mode of thinking about ways to fix the problem while trying to listen and remain present.

Brad was grateful for the assistance of his colleague who was facilitating. Over the last year, they had served as critical friends for each other. Both were trying to move from the routine of managing their schools to the active, courageous work of leading a school implementing best practices. The sessions were filled with incredible ideas and conversations. Students were telling stories of being bullied, watching bullying, and the little nagging behaviors of others that kept them from focusing on school. The teachers talked about wanting to be a part of the solution, but not knowing how.

They talked about making the hard decision to step into a situation to solve it or giving students the space to work through a tough moment. They talked about experiencing some of the same emotions as children that the students were expressing in their conversations. They wished that all schools had figured out a way to be places of comfort and kindness.

The final mixed group talked about the solutions being more simple and consistent than formal and complicated. They wanted to support people doing the right things for the right reasons as opposed to punishing those who weren't joining the community of caring. The mixed group of teachers and students did pledge that no one could be indifferent when seeing or hearing people in the community being treated unfairly.

Brad sat with his counselors and social worker to review these tapes. They were hard for the group to watch because it felt like all of their previous work in this area had been a failure. While all of the people watching the videos were working incredibly hard to convince students about the need to be kind and help others, it was clear that the coherence of the message was being lost. Brad slowly brought the concept of empathy into the conversation.

Brad felt that empathy, the ability to feel and understand what it is like to be in another person's situation, was a catalyst for treating people like you would want to be treated. It was his idea that empathy should be at the core of the proactive work in this space, but he didn't want to make the mistake of dictating ideas when he knew that the ideas fertilized by the wisdom of the room would supersede anything he brought to the table.

Brad's students were a diverse lot with as many roads to their current reality as there were kids. The counselors pointed to this diversity as a strength in the building, but they were also seeing it as a barrier to empathy as it was hard for the students to relate to the journey of the others around them. This disconnect between students caused a tension, and for the students at this school, this led to unkind words and actions. In the ugliest of moments, true bullying behavior emerged.

How do we more deeply know each other? How can we support each other every day, every minute? These two essential questions emerged for the adults at the school after watching the videotapes and spending time discussing how to build the programming needed to support the learning community's social emotional needs. With these questions, they looked to build solutions that were simple and elegant, not formal and complex, just as one student stated so wisely in a listening session.

The initial solution would have three layers of empathy building designed around the sharing of story. This started with the teachers sharing their learning journey and road to becoming a teacher. Each staff member spent fifteen to twenty minutes telling their story to colleagues about how they arrived in the current moment. This event took place during a summer staff retreat, and it was facilitated by the school social worker.

She led off the session by telling her story about why she works each day to support kids. Following all of the sharing, she talked through the best ways to facilitate these conversations with kids. She discussed ideas like how to use question prompts, how to best encourage open sharing, and how to build a physical environment that promotes the sharing of story.

The teachers took these skills back to their advisory classes to start the year. The power of sharing story at the retreat led to the staff deciding that they would spend time early in the year in double-length advisory sessions getting the learning journeys of their students on the table. In the second layer of a solution toward greater empathy, students told their stories. The student stories were shorter, but provided insight, power, and emotional attachment between the students as they listened to how life and school mixed together to make them the person that they were today.

The final piece of this three-tiered effort came from monthly gatherings where teachers and students had time and space to share additional stories about perseverance, hard work, kindness, and other traits that built the character and soul of the community. Each month, the depth and openness of these school-wide gatherings were amplified as the ecosystem of the school grew in its capacity to care.

The data were mixed for Brad and his staff. They were dealing with less bullying issues throughout the year, but it was hard to make the connection directly to these efforts to grow empathy. It did seem like there were a number of intangibles headed in the right direction. More students were wandering outside their normal groups of interaction to talk and work with others. The students were looking for ways to support each other quietly without a desire to be recognized.

The adults were showing greater empathy between each other, and it was being noticed by the students and parents. From the very beginning, Brad heard loud and clear from colleagues with experience in empathy building that consistent work in this area was the only way to make an impact. Brad knew that it wouldn't be a one-year effort to embed empathy, but it would truly need to be a lifestyle for all of those involved in this learning community.

Brad also knew that empathy was a life skill that was in growing demand in this ever evolving global community. His students and his teachers would, for the remainder of their careers, be interacting with a greater diversity of people. Understanding their story and being able to make decisions based on standing in their shoes would be essential to maximizing the change-making power of these students.

Brad had come a long way in a short time in the transformation of his school. He was energized by the changes. He was proud of the school that was growing each day. This school was different, and the students knew it. The teachers knew it. The community knew it. This led to a desire by all to push for more—more engagement, more energy for learning, and more excellence in the academic achievement of the students.

QUESTIONS FOR REFLECTION

What adult actions in your learning space are helping to build empathy?

How are you modeling empathy as a school leader?

Do students in your learning place have a sense of the concept of
empathy?

TWENTY-TWO

Slipping into the Shoes of Others

To compete in a global economy, we have no chance of outnumbering the growing planet, no chance of chasing down international test scores, and no chance of closing the borders in isolation. The greatest chance we have to compete on the global scale remains in building the next generation of learners and citizens that care more deeply than the rest of the world. We need students that care deeply each day about the issues of human dignity that trap our schools communities from realizing their potential.

The road to this possibility and greatness in our spaces of learning begins with growing empathy as a core trait of the learning ecosystem. Even the youngest of learners can begin the process of growing deep empathy by having a continuous flow of opportunities to learn about the concepts and to practice them in their daily actions.

Growing empathy and its cousin sympathy have been a part of schools in both formal and informal ways for a number of years, but a true focus on empathy (which according to Ashoka is the ability to understand the feeling and perspective of others, and to use that understanding to guide one's actions), is a growing part of the excellent learning experiences that many students around the country are beginning to have.

In schools with this focus, leaders now guide their community of learners past the place of character terms of the month and the ineffective use of external motivation, like rewards and token economies to focus on empathy. Empathy-building leaders are constructing sustainable ways to build a deep cultural story about the power of caring, listening, and understanding.

One of the leaders in supporting schools in efforts surrounding empathy building is Ashoka. This organization is designed to support social entrepreneurs throughout the world in a variety of ways. For over thirty years, Ashoka has worked to build a legion of changemakers in communities around the world, and in this effort, they have found that a core tenant of the individuals that they support is a high level of empathy. They have three thousand fellows in seventy countries that are feeding new ideas into spaces to solve problems. To support this primary mission, Ashoka is also working to ramp up the growth of a new brood of young learners into changemakers.

This includes building the "skillset and connection to purpose" needed to make this a reality. To do this, Ashoka has launched into the work of building empathy in schools. Their Smart Empathy work has started to scale, and school leaders are placing Ashoka's foundational work around empathy into their schools. Ashoka sees empathy as a "core 21st century skill" as essential as reading and math in early education. This conclusion is based on research that shows children with high levels of empathy are less likely to bully as teens.

As school leaders look to further engage their students in learning, it is essential to build empathy programming that radiates throughout the school. This programming can have the additional positive consequences of allowing more introverted students to feel comfortable in classroom conversations, supporting traditionally marginalized students to find common ground within the school, and reorienting those who spend a lot of energy on egocentric thinking and actions to have caring deeply at their core.

Leaders will also want to take this work beyond the walls of the school into the community and beyond. Doing so will allow greater freedom of thought and lower levels of stress for students as they realize that those around them in the community are also choosing words and taking actions that have empathy at the core.

Another organization working on empathy building in schools is Roots of Empathy. It started in Canada and now extends to seven countries. It is designed as a "pedagogy of hope" for children to see that their similarities can be a powerful, uniting force. The curriculum is over 639 pages long and is divided into nine themes. Each of the themes has three classroom visits as a part of its learning structure. Themes include emotional literacy, perspective taking, and inclusion.

Most schools struggle to set aside twenty-seven classroom lessons to center around empathy building, but using a triangulation of resources from places like Roots for Empathy, Ashoka, and Teaching Tolerance, school leaders can craft the right package of learning to make meaningful changes that promote students supporting students in their learning.

The Smart Empathy work by Ashoka has three parts: prepare, engage, and reflect and act. In the first area, school leaders are looking to create the conditions and school culture changes needed so empathy can thrive. These, according to the Smart Empathy program, include creating a safe space that is based on trust, leading by example (which places the actions and interactions of the adults as a model for the work that will be asked of the students), and developing emotional competency. Developing emotional competence in adults is a keystone for success in schools of empathy. Often school leaders assume that teachers naturally have these skills because of their choice of profession, but there is a need for school leaders to build capacity, including helping adults understand and manage their own emotions, in order to interpret the emotions of other adults and children. This allows more meaningful work with students to be possible.

This step alone can take multiple years to bring to a level of proficiency, but school leaders shouldn't wait to move forward into the areas of engage and reflect/act as all three phases grow in parallel as empathy in a school culture grows deeper. In the second step, students and adults are simultaneously working on activities that foster empathy and begin to uncover the power of being able to understand the feelings and perspectives of others and to use that to guide one's actions.

Ashoka provides four starting places for schools in this step. They surround the concepts of group play, storytelling, immersion, and problem solving. Ashoka is quick to point out that engagement is a locally grown concept that relies on the synergy between students, teachers, and leaders in schools to know the things that work in their space.

Play in schools has always been a time of deep informal learning. It is a time when imagination has a space to stretch and mold. It is a freedom outside of the normal structures and routines of the day, and it also promotes self-healing as kids learn to solve their own conflicts and enforce their own rules. School leaders looking to foster greater empathy have to create more time and space for students to play in a supervised but unstructured way.

Storytelling is a powerful medium for growing empathy as well. It is in knowing the stories of others that we begin to make the connections about how it would feel to be in someone else's position and place in the global ecosystem. Stories allow students to shift their mental models and see similarities and places of interconnectivity between peers, adults, and community members.

Experience allows for empathy to grow. As schools continue to race to close the achievement gap, it is often the experience gap that keeps our students from jumping across the success threshold. Students need to be immersed in the experiences of others. They need to hear, see, and be with other students and adults that are overcoming adversity, being adventurous, or looking at things differently.

Students in this step also need the opportunity to both identify and solve problems. Students who are problem identifiers have a heightened level of engagement surrounding the building of solutions to the problems that they have unearthed. By working with other students on these projects, space is created for students to overcome shared challenges and celebrate victories together, which also grows empathy.

The final piece of the Ashoka model surrounding empathy is the step of reflecting and acting. This piece helps students to internalize the empathy-building process, and it often launches fresh areas of exploration. The hope, in this stage, is that students and adults can more clearly identify shared values and differences. It is important that empathy brings a closer understanding of our core similarities as humans and participants in the global ecosystem, but it is also important that learning doesn't shy away from considering differences.

This includes naming the differences, exploring the differences, and hopefully reaching a point of respecting the differences. Acting also means empowering our students to be courageous. Students need practice with "just in time" action on issues like bullying, supporting those in need, and other moments when simple actions can change the course of the day. Students of all ages can often explain and tell peers and adults the perfect response to almost any scenario, but in the moment, these are not the actions that result. Part of breaking this barrier is to role-play, support each other in these moments, and celebrate when the courage of students is on display.

Empathy building is a habit, and habits require routines and opportunities to practice prosocial behavior. Schools that have been successful implementers of empathy as a core engagement strategy to facilitate learning are providing kids opportunity after opportunity to keep empathy at the forefront of their thinking.

At the heart of the work of leaders in schools is preparing students to be excellent citizens in this democracy. Citizens need excellent skills to reason, read, write, understand the numbers that surround them, and (it is a big *and*) connect emotionally with empathy to the world around them. They need to care so deeply that they are ready to leave this world a better place.

This deep caring starts at home, but continues throughout the learning spaces called schools. It is happening informally in so many ways, but the power of this work comes from our intentional design of space and time for students to grow their empathy and lay the foundation for becoming those that change the world.

QUESTIONS FOR REFLECTION

What levels of adult empathy are a part of the school culture? At what level do students see adult empathy in play?

Are students that are caring more learning more? If so, how do you raise the care quotient?

What platforms do students have to make a difference in their school, community and beyond?

RESOURCES

Ashoka's Start Empathy, http://startempathy.org/

Roots of Empathy, http://www.rootsofempathy.org/

Teaching Tolerance, http://www.tolerance.org/lesson/developing-empathy

Edutopia's Empathy: The Most Important Back-to-School Supply, http://www.edutopia.org/blog/empathy-back-to-school-supply-homa-tavangar

Greater Good: The Science of a Meaningful Life, http://greatergood.berkeley.edu/topic/empathy, and http://greatergood.berkeley.edu/article/item/the_politics_of_empathy

Changing Worlds, http://www.changingworlds.org

Made in the USA
Lexington, KY
18 April 2018